Meditatio
iGeneration

Meditation in the iGeneration

HOW TO MEDITATE IN A WORLD OF
SPEED AND STRESS

Andrew Holecek

Maitri Publications
Lafayette, Colorado

Maitri Publications
Meditation in the iGeneration—*How to Meditate in a World of Speed and Stress*
Andrew Holecek

For permission requests or any other questions about this publication, contact us at www.maitripublications.com.

Cover design - Cornelia G. Murariu - www.corneliagmurariu.daportfolio.com
Cover art - Cienpies Design/Thinkstock and Liufuyu/Thinkstock
Cover photo - capdesign/Thinkstock
Illustrations: Figure 1 - Vivien Mildenberger
Figures 2 & 3 - Syauqi - www.spiralkreatif.com
Final layout - ebookconverting.com

Ordering Information:
Quantity sales. Discounts are available on quantity purchases by corporations, associations, and others. For details, contact info@maitripublications.com

Meditation in the iGeneration/Andrew Holecek —1st ed.
ISBN 978-0-9897480-2-5

Contents

*This book is dedicated to John Chichester,
who taught me that the gift of truth excels all other gifts,
and whose life is the embodiment of that gift.*

Introduction

Meditation is acceptance. It is the acceptance of life within us, without us and all around us. Acceptance of life is the beginning of human satisfaction. Transformation of life is the culmination of divine satisfaction.

—Sri Chinmoy

In 1975 I was a stressed-out college student pursuing a double degree in music and biology. I put immense pressure on myself to succeed, which was a natural extension of my overachieving mentality. Ever since I was a young child I realized that attention, and therefore love, was directed towards me when I was good at something. This began with playing the piano at age five, and progressed into skiing, tennis, and my academic studies. People telling me I was good at something made me feel good. So I made it a priority, however unconscious at the time, to be good so that I could be loved.

I charged into college with this attitude, ready to conquer the world by being the best pianist on campus, the best student, and of course the best possible son. While there are many noble aspects to ambition and determination, it comes at a price and I started paying it. The stress brought me to my knees. I had a hard time sleeping, was frequently ill, and finally went to the doctor to be diagnosed with stress-induced hypertension.

The doctor gave me a handful of instructions and prescriptions to help me heal. I also started looking for ways to manage my stress without medication, and read something about the health benefits of Transcendental Meditation (TM). Studies had shown that it could reduce hypertension.[1] After mustering my courage to try something so new, I set out to learn how to meditate.

I was nervous. What is this meditation business? Could I do it? What if I failed? I didn't know anybody who meditated and had no role models. But I was stressed and sick and didn't like taking pills. I wasn't interested in spirituality or enlightenment. I just wanted to feel better.

My TM instruction was full of ritual, but I was able to see past that. The instructor was kind, the technique was simple, and the philosophy of meditation was straightforward. It was easier than I expected. Now it was up to me. Was I inspired enough—or hurting enough—to do it?

After meditating twenty minutes twice a day for just a month, my blood pressure was back to normal, I was sleeping soundly again, and my life felt balanced. I was more at ease and happier. As I continued to meditate I became a better student because I was more attentive. I found myself getting kinder. As the months clicked by I gradually realized that meditation was changing my life.

In this book I will share the miraculous power of meditation to help people like you and me. While our story lines are different, at our core we are the same. You and I both want to be happy. We want to avoid suffering. We want to find meaning and purpose in life. Joy has the same taste for both of us. Sorrow and stress and struggle have exactly the same taste for all of us. It's because we're so much more alike than we are different that I feel my story, my path in meditation, might help you with yours.

---

1 See *TM: Discovering Inner Energy and Overcoming Stress,* by Harold H. Bloomfield, MD, Michael Peter Cain, Dennis T. Jaffe, and Robert B. Kory, Delacorte Press, New York, 1975.

In 1975 there were very few books on the topic. Meditation was almost taboo, on the fringe and highly suspect. It was for people in white turbans or hippies without jobs. Since then it has entered the mainstream of our Western culture, and millions of people from prisoners to presidents now engage in some form of this ancient practice. The defense department is introducing it to marines, it is rigorously studied in neuroscience labs, the Mayo Clinic and other hospitals use it to manage chronic pain, CEO's of major corporations are employing it to increase productivity, insurance companies are realizing that meditation helps control health costs, athletes are engaging it to enhance performance, and people from all walks of life are using it to manage stress and increase happiness.

Ten different departments within the National Institutes of Health are funding dozens of studies on how meditation benefits our physical health, helping with things like heart disease, alcoholism, and menopause. Hundreds of studies have already shown the effectiveness of meditation on cancer, HIV/AIDS, rheumatoid arthritis, fibromyalgia, diabetes, attention-deficit/hyperactivity disorder, eating disorders, chronic pain, substance abuse, insomnia, psoriasis, anxiety, relapse prevention, and substance abuse— to name just a few.[2] Meditation is finding a new home in the West.

But for many people it still remains a mystery. We may know that Richard Gere and Tina Turner practice meditation, that Phil Jackson, one of the greatest NBA coaches in history, used meditation to help the Chicago Bulls and Los Angeles Lakers, that head coach Pete Carroll used meditation to help lead his Seattle Seahawks to the Super Bowl, and that the Dalai Lama, the embodiment of meditation, is a beloved world leader. But what exactly is meditation? Why should I take time out of my busy life to practice it? How can it possibly help me?

---

2 See my forthcoming book, *Fire and Ice; On the Benefits of Meditation,* for dozens of references to all these studies. Research publications on mindfulness meditation have grown from zero in 1980 to 477 in 2012.

I have been a meditation instructor for over twenty years, teaching it in churches, universities, health clubs, the federal prison system, hospices, high schools, grade schools, and many other venues. Over these two decades countless people have asked me for a good book on meditation. There are books that cover the spiritual aspects, others that deal with the physiology or psychology of meditation, and still others that provide competent nuts-and-bolts instruction. But I have yet to find a book that I can confidently refer to a corporate executive, my teenage nephews, or my mailman that covers the many facets of meditation in an accessible format. My hope is that this book meets these varied requirements. Along with its companion volume, *Fire and Ice; On the Benefits of Meditation* (which covers the mental, physical, emotional, spiritual, and social benefits) all the core aspects of meditation are explored in two short books.

In forty years of practicing and studying meditation, I have read innumerable books, attended countless retreats and seminars, and have engaged in dozens of forms of practice, including Transcendental Meditation, vipassana, yoga, Tai Chi, Qigong, Zen, Christian centering prayer, and the many practices associated with Tibetan Buddhism, including completion of the traditional three-year retreat. I have also practiced the meditative arts of calligraphy, kyudo (archery), ikebana (flower arranging), and more rigorous physical practices like trulkor and lujong (contemplative body training).

For many reasons I have settled into the Eastern contemplative traditions, primarily Buddhism. This twenty-five hundred year tradition is as viable today as it was during the time of the Buddha. Its emphasis on meditation as a way to tame the mind continues to benefit millions. Buddhism is not the only way to learn meditation, to find real happiness, or to attain enlightenment. Any tradition that offers methods to pacify the mind and open the heart is a genuine path. No one has a patent on truth—or meditation.

So even though my experience started with TM, which is based on Hindu meditative principles, and matured through Buddhist practice, it is also colored by my understanding from other philosophical and spiritual traditions, and from Western science. My mind, as well as yours, can be enhanced from the wisdom of any meditative tradition, but is also free of their limitations. I believe that what follows can help people from any tradition, or those who adhere to none at all. My aim is to present the heart of meditation in a non-sectarian way, transposing ancient wisdom into modern life, free from cultural or religious trappings, and in a user-friendly way.

When it comes to meditation, we should never mistake the map for the territory. Experience is more important than any doctrine. Study the map. Then drop it and enter the territory with a spirit of adventure. Check things out for yourself. Does meditation makes sense? Does it agree with your experience? Does it work for you? If it does, take it to heart. If it doesn't, throw it out the window. The key is to have information open your mind, not close it. As much as I honor Eastern spirituality, any authentic tradition simply points you in the right direction and invites you to make discoveries on your own. That is the approach I follow in this book.

There are a number of contemplations in the following pages. This is what brings the book to life. Contemplation is not the same as meditation, but it's a good prelude. It gathers the mind, slows it down, and directs it in. By thinking deeply about something, you're stepping on the brakes and steering your mind in the right direction. While contemplation still uses thoughts, meditation does not. As we will see, meditation allows thoughts to arise, but instead of putting them into gear and engaging them—as we would with normal thinking or even contemplating—we shift our mind into neutral. The engine of thought is still running but we're not going anywhere.

Most of us race through life in overdrive, excessively engaged in our thoughts and emotions. Contemplation is like downshifting the mind and keeping it in its lane; meditation is like taking the mind and slipping it into neutral. The mind may be humming along but we're not humming along with it. We'll have much more to say about this later.

Finally, you can read about meditation till you're blue in the face. Until you actually try it the teachings are lifeless. The most eloquent description of meditation will never approximate the experience of it. It's like trying to describe a luscious meal at the best restaurant in town. At a certain point you just have to go and taste it for yourself. The brief contemplations are appetizers for the main meal. If you like their flavor they will nourish your experience and whet your appetite for meditation. They are designed to bring the material from your head down into your heart, and then into daily life.

My hope is that you eventually put this book about meditation aside, just as you would return any menu, and savor your own experience of it.

CHAPTER 1

What's the Problem?

Meditation is a magnificent tool practiced for thousands of years, across dozens of cultures, by millions of people. But a tool for what? What's the problem? Why should I meditate? If you wake up in the middle of the night in total contentment, survey your life with complete satisfaction, and find yourself stress free, then maybe you don't need meditation. If you don't have a question there's no need for an answer. The first step in solving a problem is realizing there is one.

But if you're young and stressed about school, getting a job, or being successful, then meditation can help. If you're older and worry about your kids, your retirement, your relationships, or the economy, meditation can help. If you're anywhere in between and trying to find more meaning in life, to live it more fully, to be more focused, or to discover real happiness, then meditation can help.

People today are hurting. The litany of personal, social, and global problems is obvious. While this book can help with these larger issues, it's meant to help us with our personal ones. When you get down to it, global problems are by-products of personal issues. People, not the physical world itself, cause most of the world's difficulties. The Christian philosopher Blaise Pascal said; "All of man's difficulties are caused by his inability to sit, quietly, in a room by himself." Our journey will take us to the root of our difficulties, and show us how to sit quietly by ourselves to remedy them.

On an individual level, there are many sources of discontent. You've probably heard them all. One of the most noticeable, and unsettling, is the epidemic of distraction, busyness, and speed. Emails are popping up constantly on our iPhones, droids, and laptops. They often spawn a sense of urgency—I need to read it and respond *now*. Text messages ping into our awareness endlessly, commanding an instant reply. Facebook and Twitter are conquering the world, and our attention. Information is hurled at us from every conceivable direction, and at speeds that are reaching escape velocity from reality.

The result of this relentless barrage is people like you and me. Innocent folks who are being drawn and quartered by the dark side of this information age. Our minds are being torn apart and scattered in all directions as we struggle to keep up with a world that is running out of control. We're losing touch—with ourselves, with others, and with reality. Tools that are designed to connect us (the social network, the world wide web) pull us away from human contact. How many times have you seen people at a dinner table relating more to their devices than to each other? How often have you been distracted while reading this chapter? Gadgets made to simplify our life are making it more complex. Smart phones are dumbing us down. Every new upgrade serves to downgrade our attention span. Convenience has turned into a bill of rights, and instant gratification is virtually law.

A recent study at Carnegie Mellon showed that the distraction of an interruption made test takers 20 percent dumber. That's enough to turn a B- student (80 percent) into a failure (62

percent).[3] Even the names given to the contraptions of this information age, which is also the age of interruption or distraction
technology, hint at the problem. "Droid" (the smart phones that
aren't iPhones) is short for "android," which means "an automaton
in the form of a human being." "Twitter" means "to talk lightly
and rapidly, especially of trivial matters" and often instills a "state
of tremulous excitement." "Facebook" mostly delivers face value,
and struggles with conveying depth. "Surfing" the web denotes
skimming across the surface of things; the internet and world
wide web imply getting caught up; something going "viral" sug-
gests a rapidly spreading infection; iPhones, iPads, iPods, iTunes,
iMovie, iChat, and iCal are all about "I," not you. And all these flat
screens depict a superficial life with the ultimate depth of a pixel.
It's a perfect symbol of how the information age is screening us
from life—and making everything flat.

Our speedy and splintered lives are like a stone tossed across
the surface of a pond. We skip from one bit of information to the
next, as fast as possible, with no ultimate goal in sight. We're glanc-
ing on top of life, going nowhere fast. And we're outsourcing our
mental capacities to slippery silicon chips, then wondering why
our personal lives don't compute any more. One of the biggest
problems is that we confuse information for experience, and end
up existing in a virtual world. We live in our head and not in reality.

The clinical result of this speed is what professionals call
continuous partial attention, attention deficit disorder (ADD), attention deficit hyperactivity disorder (ADHD), or any number of
infections of attention. We're neither fully here nor there. Below
this surface diagnosis lurk depression, anxiety disorders, and a
host of deeper problems.[4] The opposite of evolution is *devolution,*

---

3 See *Brain, Interrupted* by Bob Sullivan and Hugh Thompson, in *The New York Times,*
May 5th, 2013.
4 For example, studies have shown that those with ADHD have much higher rates of
criminality and drug abuse. See Paul Lichtenstein of the Karolinska Institute in Stock-
holm, quoted in *The Denver Post,* November 22, 2012.

and distraction is at the heart of that treacherous regression. (See Figure 1 below.)

Figure 1
Evolution and Devolution

We're choosing information overload, divided attention, and multi-tasking, and losing our ability to concentrate, contemplate, or introspect. Thoreau referred to the technological marvels of his day as "improved means to an unimproved end." How much more "marvelous" are these modern gadgets, and how dramatically unimproved is the end today? These technological marvels are often nothing more than weapons of mass distraction, and just as destructive as their military counterparts.

The personal result of distraction and speed is a gnawing feeling of dissatisfaction, anxiety, and loss of meaning and purpose. There's a sense that something is missing. Life feels incomplete. As we will see, something *is* missing. But it's not out there. What's missing is in here. Our attention is missing. We've gone AWOL on reality. We're all MIA—missing in attention. As the song says: we're looking for love—and happiness—in all the wrong places. It's such an irony: our inability to be fully present (in here) is what generates the sense of absence (out there)—a topic we will return to in detail.

There's no shortage of bad news. We all know it. While there's no need to harp about it, there is a need to identify it. Without a proper diagnosis we'll never find a cure. We'll continue to speed along with everybody else, feeling the pressure to keep up, and find ourselves more and more dissatisfied. I rented a U-Haul truck the other day and right above the speedometer was this safety message, a lesson that applies to all of life: "Speed kills. Slow down and live longer." Mental speediness—the zoom zone of the modern mind—kills the deeper experience of life. Slow down and live more fully. Reboot your soul into silence and stillness.

Studies have shown that many people are turning to drugs or alcohol to manage their stress.[5] Others are turning to entertainment, or infinite forms of addicting distraction (addiction itself is a form of distraction). Perhaps one solution is some digital detox. Perhaps the best solution is to temporarily drop out. Not out of life, like a hippie, but out of our busyness and speed. Take a few minutes to drop out of each day and into a peaceful state called meditation. Take a break. Stop skipping across the surface of life and you may find the depth that you seek. You may find what's missing. Stop and drop—into the magic of meditation.

Without taking an honest look at our lives, and the suffering of others, we tend to grow numb and complacent. So many people are insensitive—literally and figuratively out of touch—with themselves and with others. Because they spend so much time in their distracted heads they're losing the ability to feel, and to empathize. Perhaps it's because things in the real world are so bad that we take refuge in a virtual one. It's so easy and tempting to check out of reality and into a flat screen—either a literal one, or the screen of our distracting thoughts and fantasies. But if we

5 See *Managing Stress: Principles and Strategies for Health and Wellbeing* by Brian Luke Seaward, Jones and Bartlett Learning, Burlington, MA, 2012.

continue to check out, the world will continue to go viral. And we will all merrily skip our way into personal and collective hell.

Distraction doesn't just kill the full experience of the present moment—it literally kills. How many times have we heard about some tragic accident because a driver or pedestrian was inattentive? How many times a day do we bump into things, physically or psychologically, because we are mindless? All these small accidents are ominous warnings of the impending larger ones.

Distracted people don't notice things. They don't perceive the clear and present danger because they're not present for it.[6] As the poet Rumi said, "Sit down and be quiet. You are drunk and this is the edge of the roof."

The frog

It's akin to what happened to that poor distracted frog. If you take a frog and place it in room temperature water, it will bathe in comfort. Life is good for the frog, if not a bit sleepy. If you slowly raise the temperature of the water, the frog will never take notice. The heat is on but he doesn't feel it. The frog has acclimatized to a climate that is almost literally going to hell. Before he has time to jump out he will be boiled alive. Because the temperature changes were so gradual, and because he adapted to them, he never knew what hit him. He adapted his way out of existence.

Adaptation has its place, but it's not humane to adapt to mass shootings to the point where the next one seems par for the course. It's not healthy to acclimatize to increasingly deadly hurricanes, super storms, or raging wildfires as if they were normal. It's not in our evolutionary interest to adapt to rising instances of corruption, animal cruelty, or corporate greed. It's not safe to

---

6 In 2011, 23% of auto accidents involved cell phones, which equals 1.3 million crashes. Texting while driving makes a crash up to twenty-three times more likely. See www.textinganddrivingsafety.com/texting-and-driving-stats/

adapt to air pollution so bad you can't see the top of skyscrapers. This kind of adaptation is born from growing numb. Anesthesia is good for surgery. It's not good for life. Growing numb means growing dumb.

Despite what Darwin says, adaptation is not always the best way to survive and evolve. Sometimes we need to wake up and revolt. The meditation revolution, because it's a revolution in awareness, is a sane and gentle way to do that.

Whether it's the unsettling climate of our lives, or that of the world, things are heating up. As Al Gore put it, the world has a fever—and so do we. Physical, mental, and environmental inflammation is epidemic. Global warming—at every level—is real. The good news is that unlike that doomed frog, sensitive people are starting to squirm. They're looking for ways to cool off.

As we will see, meditation is a form of internal climate control. It's a mental and behavioral anti-inflammatory that quells the emotional fires within. It allows us to chill out personally and to start to calm the world down collectively. Unlike its physical counterparts (like ibuprofen), this mental anti-inflammatory is totally organic and natural. Meditation simply returns us to our natural, balanced, and cool state of being.

Studies have shown how harmful physical inflammation is, which is why the anti-inflammatory business is a multi-billion dollar industry. Left unchecked, inflammation leads to a host of diseases, from simple rashes and acne, to the epidemic of allergies, autoimmune disorders like arthritis, even heart disease and cancer. It can lead to wrinkles and pre-mature aging. Inflammation is like a smoldering fire that ignites all sorts of disease. The scary thing about inflammation is that it can be going on inside us like a coal fire and we'll never know it—*because we can't feel it.* We're out of touch with our inner physical selves and can't feel the burn.

Unlike the overheated frog, the "hot water" is not only outside of us (global warming), but also within (inflammation).

These inflammatory processes are also happening within us at mental and psychological levels. We're equally out of touch with our mental and emotional selves, and the "heat" that is generated at those levels. One consequence of mental speed is mental heat. There's so much internal friction with our racing thoughts that people worldwide are at the boiling point. Can you sense it? From road rage, to political spats, to celebrity duels, to workplace shootings, to domestic violence—hot heads abound. Because the baseline emotional temperature is so high, a single inflammatory comment or event can tip a person, or an entire country, into exploding.

Research has shown that as temperatures rise, tempers flare. One report states, "Many global climate models project global temperature increases of at least 3.6 degrees Fahrenheit over the next half century. Our results imply that if nothing changes, this rise in temperature could amplify the rate of group conflicts like civil wars by an astonishing 50 percent in many parts of the world—a frightening possibility for a planet already awash in conflict."[7] This is a startling indicator of the relationship between outer and inner inflammatory processes.

We'll have more to say about inflammation later.[8] The point here is that we're in serious hot water. Until we're forced to take note of it, which usually happens when it boils over into physical disease, social dis-ease, or emotional unrest, we remain unaware of the simmering heat within. Meditation douses behavioral inflammation at its root. By slowing the mind it reduces the rub—and prevents all manner of overheating.

---

7 See *Weather and Violence*, by Marshall Burke, Solomon Hsiang, and Edward Miguel, in *The New York Times*, Sept. 1st, 2013.

8 *Fire and Ice; On the Benefits of Meditation* devotes entire chapters to this hot topic.

The good news

There is a silver lining in this cloud of personal and global unease. If we acknowledge the bad news, and relate to it intelligently, it leads to good news. Diagnosis leads to cure. When something isn't working we start to ask questions. Is there an alternative? Is there something that can help me? Is there a way out? The way out, in this case, is to find our way in. The revolution is internal. It's an attention revolution.

If we can find our way in, we will return to our center. We will recapture the cool balance that is our birthright and that balance will spread to the world. So if you're feeling off center, dissatisfied, and out of touch, that's good news. You're getting in touch with the scratchy truth. This awareness can spur you to find something that will help you feel centered again.

I often teach meditation in religious and spiritual centers, and they humorously tell me that business is good. Not in a greedy way, of course, but because it means people are searching. Whether it's for answers, meaning, happiness, or relief. Something is off and people know it.

For many people meditation may be an answer. But we have to be careful. While it's possible for meditation to be the solution, we need to be realistic. To view meditation as a panacea is to guarantee disappointment. There are two extreme ways people relate to meditation, both of which lead to failure. Some skeptics are so doubtful about meditation that it becomes a self-fulfilling prophecy. They try it half-heartedly and it doesn't work. Others are so enthusiastic about it that it also doesn't work. They drop it when expectations aren't met. While meditation is a remarkable tool, don't burden it with excessive doubt or hope.

A common theme in this book is that of the "middle way." Here that means not getting stuck in the extremes of doubt or hope. A little skepticism is healthy, but don't close your mind. A little enthusiasm is also healthy, but don't get manic. The best approach is to keep an open but questioning attitude. Try it and see if it works.

You may feel so busy that you're leery about adding anything new to your life. You just don't have time to meditate. Meditation is to help you slow down and relax, not to add further speed and stress. While it does take some time and effort, meditation is really about subtracting things from your life. It adds to your life by taking needless things away from it.

As meditation takes you below the surface of life and into more meaningful depths, you begin to let go of those things that don't really matter. It simplifies your life. This is where it is a kind of panacea. Your meditative mind will reach deep into you, curing the ailments associated with frivolity and speed. It's frequently referred to as medicine for the soul, a restorative balm. Meditation as medication gets a lot of humorous press.

Meditation can increase your happiness and heighten your awareness. It can instill strength of mind, openness of heart, and inner peace. Sogyal Rinpoche, a modern meditation master, says, "Learning to meditate is the greatest gift you can give yourself in this life. For it is only through meditation that you can undertake the journey to discover your true nature, and so find the stability and confidence you will need to live, and die, well."

But we're getting ahead of ourselves. Let's define it first.

CHAPTER 2

What is Meditation—Part One

Because there are so many different forms of meditation, there are a number of ways to define it. It's important to have a clear definition, and therefore a clear understanding. If your definition is too narrow you will end up judging yourself based on that definition, and sabotage your practice. A narrow definition would be something like, "Meditation means getting rid of thoughts. If I'm having thoughts I'm not meditating." That definition will make you miserable. Who can meditate without having thoughts?

If your definition is too wide, meditation loses meaning. Everything, and therefore nothing, becomes meditation. A too wide definition would be, "My walk this morning was my meditation." That could be, if you were applying the technique of mindful walking. But if taking the walk just got your mind off your problems, it's not really meditating. If your mindfulness (which is the ability to be fully present) is completely developed, which means you're mindful in everything you do, then everything can become your meditation. But that's more advanced.

If your definition is simply wrong, you will unknowingly use a twisted measuring stick to evaluate your meditation and spin off in the wrong direction. You would see yourself as if looking at a circus mirror, which gives a warped reflection. Chapter Four will list a number of wrong definitions—what meditation is not—to keep you from deforming your meditation practice.

Meditation is habituating to openness. It's about opening your mind, and making room for any thought or emotion that arises within it. While there are certainly wrong definitions of meditation, the proper definition, like the practice itself, should be similarly open. I've been meditating for thirty-seven years and my definition is continually being refined as my understanding deepens.

Most people have narrow definitions, which closes their minds and pinches their practice. For example, many people think that the only posture for meditation is sitting crossed legged on a cushion. That's just one way to do it. You can meditate lying down, standing, or even walking. Once you get the hang of it, you can meditate anywhere and anytime. That's when your walk does become your meditation.

It's best to err on the side of keeping an open and wide definition, and therefore an open evaluation of how you are doing when you actually meditate. You will judge yourself against your definition, so be generous and accurate. Meditation teacher Norman Fischer offers this advice:

> [I]f you are meditating in the morning feeling half asleep, with dream-snatches passing by, and your mind not crisply focused precisely on the breath, the way you think it is supposed to be ... this is perfectly all right. It is considered normal, and even beneficial... Evaluate your practice on a much wider and more generous calculus. Not: Is my mind concentrated while I am sitting? But: After meditating in the morning, how is my attention during the day? Not: Am I peaceful and still as I sit? But: Is my habit of flying off the

handle reducing somewhat? In other words, the test of meditation isn't meditation. It's your life. [9]

As with any discipline, it may take awhile for some of these effects to take place in your life, but this is where to look to evaluate your practice. You may feel that your meditation isn't productive, which is a common mistake, but then you begin to notice that you're more patient or kind. You realize you're listening better, or more aware of the aroma of your coffee. You're less distracted. These are just a few of the many indicators that something is happening. The mirror of meditation isn't as tiny as your formal practice sessions. It's as wide as the rest of your life.

As we will see, the technique of meditation provides a canvas, a background, upon which you can paint and observe your mind. The technique allows you to see things you haven't seen before. It's not meant to provide a measuring stick, or something to beat yourself up with. It's so easy to think something like, "I'm supposed to follow my breath. I can't do that. I'm always distracted. I can't meditate." We inadvertently use the meditation technique to judge and criticize ourselves. If the technique is held that way, meditation becomes just another thing we can't live up to.

Many people use their definitions to rate and then berate themselves. This is an irony because meditation is about dropping all judgments. When they do rate themselves they usually come up short. They feel they can't measure up to the demands of meditation, and don't realize those demands are self-imposed. So they quit. *Not because their meditation is off, but because their definition is.*

I had a student this week tell me, "I suck at sitting." After talking to him I discovered that his meditation is fine. It's his definition that sucks. So a healthy definition is really important, which is why the next three chapters are devoted to this topic.

---

9 Shambhala Sun Magazine, September 2010, Volume 19, Number 1. "Getting Started," p. 76.

Mindfulness

The most basic form of meditation is *mindfulness*. This is where we start. Mindfulness is undivided attention to the present moment, to what's happening *now*, without conceptual elaboration or emotional reactivity. Zen master Thich Nhat Hanh calls mindfulness a miracle. If your goal is to calm your mind and bring peace to your life, this miraculous practice is for you. Mindfulness is like taking a choppy lake and settling it into a mirror-like surface. Instead of being tossed around by the wind and waves of life, your mind floats serenely on tranquil waters.

The waves are our distracting thoughts and emotions. Once they settle down, so does the sediment (our confusion and misery) churned up by those waves. Our thoughts and emotions are gradually pacified. The inner and outer world becomes clearer. We become aware of things and thoughts never seen before. This is the second part of meditation, which is the cultivation of *awareness*. *Mindfulness—awareness* always complement each other, and they are the heart of our journey. They also reinforce each other. With meditation we're replacing the vicious circle of speed and stress with the virtuous circle of mindfulness and awareness. We will discuss mindfulness in this chapter and awareness in the next.

Mindfulness meditation goes back thousands of years, well before the time of Christ, the Buddha, or any forefather of modern religion. The Buddha used mindfulness because of its simplicity and power, but it was not his invention. Mindfulness is the art of taming the mind by gently returning it to the present moment. It's common to many traditions. How to actually do it is presented in Chapter Six.

If you close your eyes and look at your mind you will discover that it's constantly filled with thoughts. That's just what the normal mind does—it thinks. One moment you're thinking about tomorrow, in the next you're reflecting about yesterday. There's the thought of what your co-worker said, quickly replaced by a memory of the weekend, that switches into the thought of having to pick up some milk. This is *mindlessness*, the opposite of mindfulness, and it's rampant in the modern world. Everybody is constantly thinking, fantasizing, or worrying. Everybody is on automatic pilot, sleep walking through life. When you drove home today, or took a walk, how much were you actually present for that drive or walk? How much of your life is filled with idle thought? That's mindlessness.

Contemplation—What do you see?

Most of us never look at our mind. Perhaps the closest experience is going to sleep at night, or waking up in the morning and languishing in bed. At those times our thoughts and emotions stand out, but have you ever really looked at them? What do you see when you look at your mind? Take a few minutes now and look. Are you inquisitive, or does this make you uneasy? Does one thought or feeling flow right into the next? Is there any space between your thoughts? When you look, don't try to change anything. Like a good reporter doing a travelogue on a new country, notice whatever appears without judging it.

These rambling thoughts and emotions have tremendous power. They rule our lives. We go to the fridge because we first have the thought of doing so. We get a job, propose to a mate, read a book, take a trip, or play tennis all because we had a thought or emotion that propelled us. Look at your life and you will discover that thoughts and emotions are the spark plugs that drive the engine of your experience. The mind—our thoughts and emotions—leads all things.

Sometimes the contents of our mind are so intense we can't go to sleep, or we grind our teeth and get an ulcer. Sometimes our feelings are so overwhelming that we do things that get us in trouble. Just read the morning paper to see the results of mindlessness at work. People get themselves into all kinds of situations because of what they think and feel. As meditation will show you, the only power thoughts really have is the power we give them. Left alone, they are harmless energy bubbles of the mind.

Imagine taking an untamed Great Dane for a walk on a leash. If you're not strong, the dog will probably take you for a walk! He will tug you to the right to sniff out some garbage, pull you off to the left to pee against a tree, and knock you off balance as he chases a cat. In the same way, our thoughts and emotions pull us to and fro. A thought arises, or an emotion flares, and unless we relate to it properly we will chase it like a dog running after a stick. Unless we take control of them, our thoughts and emotions take control of us. But unlike reigning in a frisky dog, with meditation we don't tighten the leash to control our mind. As we'll see, we cut the leash to free both our thoughts and ourselves.

Contemplation - What is it that moves you?

The next time you do something (like take a break from this book), look to see what triggers that action. Is there a thought or feeling that caused you to move? Why do you do what you do? This contemplation can bring insight not only into your present actions, but also to your entire life. Without reflection, most of us live our lives chasing the proverbial carrot on the stick, either the ones we provide for ourselves or that advertisers provide for us. All those thoughts and images are carrots luring us forward. Are there moments when an action is not propelled by a thought or emotion?

The natural power of presence

These wandering thoughts and emotions not only run our lives, they also dilute our experience. It's like the static of a radio station not quite tuned in. There's all this interference in our mind that detracts from the beauty of being fully present. When thinking goes up, awareness goes down.

A few days ago I took my favorite hike to a viewpoint that looks out at the continental divide. It was a day before an important business meeting. When I first reached the viewpoint I was struck by the snow capped peaks and the crisp mountain air. The power of the scenery tuned me in to the present moment and brought me fully to life. But within a few minutes I started thinking about the meeting. I was worried about not being prepared, thinking about what my boss would say, what my co-workers might think, what the result of my presentation might be. Ten minutes later I "woke up" and realized I had completely tuned out of where I was. My experience of the present moment was watered-down by my thoughts about tomorrow. This was an example of how mindlessness constantly dilutes our experience. My body was at the viewpoint, but my mind was viewing the meeting. You can't be in two places at the same time—even though we try. You can't multi-task on reality. As the Roman philosopher Seneca said, "To be everywhere is to be nowhere."

Mindfulness is being totally dialed in, one hundred percent present. It's the formal practice of non-distracted awareness. Being mindful is being present in your experience without judging right or wrong, good or bad. It's the precision of being attentive to details, of being on the dot. The architect Mies van der Rohe said, "God is in the details." Finding "God," or at least the freedom of being in the moment, is therefore a consequence of mindfulness. The Devil, of course, is distraction.

Mindlessness is being partly here and partly there, which results in partial presence. Whether we know it or not, most of us train in partial presence, or mindlessness, every day. Every time we give in to distraction we're practicing mindlessness. Which means we practice it all the time. But because we're so used to being distracted, we just don't see it. T. S. Elliot wrote, "We are distracted from distraction by distraction." Instead of *coming back* to the present moment, we're always *breaking away* from it.

Fractured attention is what gives birth to that feeling that something's missing. According to one study, we're distracted about 47% of the time.[10] That means that we're missing out on nearly half of our lives. No wonder we feel that something is missing.

We multi-task, speed from one event to another, and are bombarded with infinite forms of information or distraction. Because of this combination of busyness and speed, we've become masters of mindlessness. And because we've been mindless for so long, it feels like the natural state. But it's not. Mindlessness is a state we have trained ourselves into.

Mindfulness is the natural state. Which is why it feels so honest and good. It's like coming home. After a long day of running errands, or weeks of traveling—of going, going, going—you finally return home and breathe a sigh of relief. That's what mindfulness feels like. The ineffable sense of dissatisfaction that we often feel is a form of homesickness. We're homesick for this natural state.

The practice of mindfulness may not feel natural at first, only because we're so adept at mindlessness, but being present is our authentic state of being. This is why some teachers use the term "attention deficit disorder" for mindlessness, because it really is a disorder. Our scattered minds are "out of order" in both senses of that phrase: they aren't working properly, and they're off-centered. The center, of course, is the present moment. Mindfulness brings us back to the center, and reinstates that natural order.

We don't see mindlessness as a disorder because most everyone is infected with it. It's the new normal, something we've

---

10 See *A Wandering Mind is an Unhappy Mind*, by Matthew A. Killingsworth and Daniel T. Gilbert, *Science*, Vol. 330, Nov. 2010.

dangerously adapted to. Mindlessness seems natural. It may be the natural by-product of this crazy age, but it's not the natural state of our mind. This is an important point because it initially takes effort to train our mind to be fully present. In other words, mindfulness practice may seem unnatural at first. It can be initially difficult. But if we have the view that mindfulness is natural, that once we remove our mindless habits, mindfulness naturally shines, we can prevent a lot of frustration.

The point is this: *We're not trying to cultivate anything artificial in mindfulness meditation.* Even though it may seem that way. We're trying to reveal the natural state of our mind.[11]

This also means that most of the effort comes up front. Flipping from mindlessness to mindfulness is like flowing along with the current of a rapidly moving river, then deciding to row upstream to reach the tranquil headwaters. Once you reach the headwaters you can relax in its stillness. Until then it takes work. There's all this momentum to counteract, the current of so many habits created by a lifetime of distraction. You won't feel the force of distraction if you continue to go with the flow. Keep giving in to the impulse to check your smart phone, email, or text messages and you'll never feel the force of mindlessness. But once you start to meditate and turn against the flow, the impact of distraction is finally felt.

Adapting to the mindless flow may be easier, but it's lethal. Acclimatization to distraction and speed is the source of so much trouble. And it's accelerating. The flow has turned into deadly rapids, and it's flushing us towards a perilous future.

---

11 This statement is at odds with what neuroscientists assert. Scientists studying mindfulness claim that mindlessness is the natural state. But this is a presumptive claim, based on their limited population pool. In other words, they are looking at a population that has already trained themselves into mindlessness. They are studying people who are virtuosos in mindlessness—because they've been unwittingly practicing it for a long time. The contemplative traditions are unequivocal: the natural mind is always mindful.

The good news is that your initial enthusiasm for meditation is usually strong enough to get you past this turning point. Switching metaphors, once you get the ball rolling, it gets easier and easier. At the summits of meditation, mindfulness becomes totally effortless, which makes sense because mindfulness is the natural state.

Here's more good news: if there's one word that summarizes the meditative journey, it is *relaxation*. Relax into the present moment; relax into the natural order of things. Instead of always struggling to make things happen, we can let things happen. Instead of racing to keep up, we can give it up. A relaxed mind is a mindful mind.

Working hard to relax is therefore the great irony of meditation. Even though mindfulness is the natural state, it takes effort to uncover that state. On one hand it seems like we're taming and then training the mind, but on the other hand we're just revealing its innate qualities. If we just leave the mind alone, it is naturally present and aware. But the trick is that we have to leave it alone properly. Leaving it alone doesn't mean letting it roam wherever it wants. That's just daydreaming, another form of mindlessness. Leaving it alone means learning how to let the mind relax into its natural state—which wakes us up from our daydreams. It's about being present with awareness. That is the art of meditation.

Presenting this important point at the beginning sets the stage for all the details that follow, and that are all designed to help us relax. While the details and work of meditation are important, don't let them trip you up or intimidate you. Rest your mind in its natural present state and you will have accomplished mindfulness.

Mindfulness and happiness

As simple as mindfulness is, it has deep and surprising applications. We will explore many throughout the book. Here is a big one: mindfulness is at the root of happiness. As sociologist Erik Fromm said, "Man misses the only satisfaction that can give him real happiness—the experience of the activity of the present moment."

Mindfulness is having a mind-full-of-nowness. Nowness is where life happens. It doesn't happen in the past or the future, which is where our thinking mind spends most of its time as we think about something that may happen, or remember something that already did. So meditation brings us fully into life by bringing us fully into the present moment. A friend recently told me, "If you have one foot in the future and the other in the past, you're pissing on the present." Don't piss your life away. Plant both feet here and now.

Contemplation - The common denominator of happiness

Recall several moments when you were really happy. Maybe it was when you graduated, or got your first job. Perhaps it was when you were playing with your children, or watching a dazzling sunset. Perhaps it was the moment you got married, received a promotion, or bought your new house. Now reflect further on whether there was a common denominator behind all these experiences. Is there something shared in every experience of happiness?

If you do this contemplation you'll discover that one of the common ingredients behind happiness is being fully present. When you're having a great time with your friends it's not because you're thinking about tomorrow or mulling over yesterday. It's because you're fully there with your friends. If you're sipping a latte and quietly content, it's because you're there for the taste and aroma of the latte.

The only difference between these familiar examples of happiness, and the happiness cultivated by meditation, is that the former are conditional and the latter is unconditional. In other words, even though the ingredient behind any form of happiness is complete presence, the way we get there is different. Normally, we find ourselves happy when certain conditions come together. Whether it's the condition of hanging out with our friends, watching a sunset, or drinking a latte, some set of external circumstances brings us to nowness and we find ourselves happy.

The problem with this form of happiness is that because we come to associate happiness with certain conditions, we then spend much of our life trying to replicate these conditions. We become slaves to external circumstance. I was happy when [fill in the blank], so let's try to [fill in the blank] again. When we set out to repeat those conditions and they're not met, instead of finding happiness we find frustration. The latte wasn't hot enough or it was too sweet. Clouds obscured the sunset or other people were at our favorite spot. Conditional happiness is always temporary because when the conditions fade so does the happiness.

Meditation cultivates unconditional, and therefore lasting, happiness. It does so by bringing us into nowness, but without the restrictions of external circumstance. When you train your mind to rest in the present, it doesn't matter what happens in the world. A lukewarm latte? No problem. I'll relate to it properly and enjoy it just as it is. A cloud over my sunset? No big deal. Let's celebrate that. Near the end of his long life, the Indian sage Krishnamurti was asked about the secret to his enduring happiness. His reply spoke to the heart of mindfulness: "I don't mind what happens."

This is the fruit of meditation. Only seasoned meditators dwell in mindfulness most of the time, so don't despair. Most meditators reach this state now and then, and patiently work towards the goal of being mindful as much as possible. But just knowing this is possible can inspire you to accomplish mindfulness, and therefore discover the secret to real happiness. And it's free! The only thing you have to pay is attention. You only have to bring your attention, over and over, back to nowness.

This is why some of the happiest people are those who are free from external trappings. They don't need a stock portfolio or a Porsche to be happy. They have discovered that real wealth and happiness comes from within. It's an inside job. This is also why some of the most miserable people are those who seem to have everything. Because they think a car or house or fame or fortune brings happiness, they clamor for more of those conditions. But instead of happiness they find hassle. Instead of freedom they find traps. The poet John Milton, in his book appropriately called *Paradise Lost*, said:

> The mind is its own place, and in itself
> Can make a Heaven of Hell, a Hell of Heaven

"Paradise Found" is discovered by those who realize that heaven or hell is not out there. Heaven or hell is a state of mind, not a state in external reality. Paradise is found within. This simple maxim carries thermonuclear power. It really is the secret to happiness. But simple does not mean easy. To make a heaven of hell requires practice, and mindfulness is the first step in that practice.

Mindfulness shows you that happiness is your responsibility. Nobody can make you happy or sad. Only you have that power. There's no person or thing that will always make you smile or frown. A few years ago I was sent this lovely story, a tale of paradise found:

> The 92-year old, petite, well-poised and proud lady, who is fully dressed each morning by eight o'clock, with her fashionably coifed and makeup perfectly applied, even though she is legally blind,

moved to a nursing home today. Her husband of 70 years recently passed away, making the move necessary.

After waiting patiently in the lobby of the nursing home, she smiled sweetly when told her room was ready. As she maneuvered her walker to the elevator, I provided a visual description of her tiny room, including eyelet sheets that had been hung on her window. "I love it," she stated with the enthusiasm of an eight-year old having just been presented with a new puppy.

"Mrs. Jones," I said, "you haven't seen the room. Just wait."

"That doesn't have anything to do with it," she replied. "Happiness is something you decide on ahead of time. Whether I like the room or not doesn't depend on how the furniture is arranged. It's how I arrange my mind. I already decided to love it. It's a decision I make every morning when I wake up. I have a choice. I can spend the day in bed recounting the difficulty I have with the parts of my body that no longer work, or get out of bed and be thankful for the ones that do."

She then gave these five rules to be happy:

1. Free your heart from hatred.
2. Free your mind from worries.
3. Live simply.
4. Give more.
5. Expect less.

Because she was able to arrange her mind properly, it didn't matter what kind of arrangements were provided by the world. She had already found her paradise.

Mindfulness and love

Mindfulness is about proper attendance, and showing up for your life. For some people it may seem cold and almost clinical, a purely mental practice. But mindfulness is equally defined as *heartfulness*.

"Mind" and "heart" is the same word in Pali, *citta,* and in Sanskrit, *chitta.* In Tibet, when someone talks about their mind they point to their heart, not their head. The Chinese character for "mindfulness" combines the ideograms for presence and heart. And the Japanese character for mindfulness is composed of two figures, one represents mind, the other, heart. The Sufi teacher Hazrat Inayat Kahn said, "The mind is the surface of the heart, the heart the depth of the mind."

The tendency to associate mindfulness with mental exercise contributes to the misunderstanding that meditation means escaping into some disembodied headspace. Meditators are sometimes accused of being disconnected from reality, "staring at their navels" or "lost in inner (mental) space." There is some truth to this accusation, which arises from an improper understanding of meditation. As we will see throughout this book, real meditation is more about heart than head.

To attend to something properly means to tend to it, to care for it. When you care for something, you're naturally mindful towards it, and when you're mindful towards something, you naturally care for it. This is how mindfulness naturally ex-tends to the rest of the world, and brings about care for it. "Attention" is connected to the word "tend," and also to "tender." The tenderness developed in meditation often surprises people who think meditation is just a head game. Zen teacher John Tarrant said, "Attention is the most basic form of love."

Look at an object in front of you. If you can, hold it in your hands. Tend to it for a moment. Give it your undivided attention. Notice how this evokes a quality of caring. Notice how your full attendance opens your heart towards the object. As your mind becomes full of the object, so does your heart. Mindfulness really means carefulness, or care-fullness. You spontaneously start to care for things, starting with your own mind, then extend that care towards others.

There's a scene in the movie *Siddartha* where the central character picks up a rock and says, "I love this rock." It's not because he has rocks in his head. He's not crazy. It's because his complete attention allows him to see the completeness and beauty of the rock. He tends to the rock fully, and this tenderness brings out the natural purity and goodness of the rock—or anything else he attends to. He has taken the rock to heart, so I suppose we could say he has rocks in his heart, but that's a good thing—and a spontaneous expression of his heartfulness.

Contemplation - The miracle of taste

Take a grape (or raisin, blackberry etc.), hold it between your fingers. Bring your undivided attention to the grape. Take a full minute to feel its texture, coolness, and shape. Slowly bring it to your lips, almost kiss it. Let your lips feel its texture, coolness, and shape. Put it on your tongue and play with it for a minute before biting into it. Have you ever felt a grape this way before? Now bite into it, mindfully. Feel the moisture, really taste it. Mindfulness is literally sensual. It can make you a better lover—of anything. Take another minute to chew it. Celebrate the magic of this fruit; revel in the wonder of mindful eating. Swallow it. Appreciate what nature has just given you. Try this once a day for a few days, and see what happens. Does it change your relationship to food? Do you taste things differently?

Conversely, mindlessness is also heartlessness. It gives birth to carelessness, a lack of tending. When you're careless about something you're naturally mindless towards it, and when you're mindless towards something you naturally care less for it. When we're mindless we often hurt others. Instead of embracing and including others with heartfulness, we reject and exclude them in a heartless way. Our lack of attention actually damages the world.

Look at the difference between someone who's speedy and plagued with mindlessness, and someone who's slow and steady with mindfulness. The former stomps on the world, the latter treads lightly upon it. Opening your heart, walking care-fully through life, and falling more easily in love with everything is a magnificent consequence of the practice of heartfulness.

This heart aspect of meditation lends itself beautifully to the many discoveries that arise in meditation, especially when we enter the second phase of *awareness*. George Washington Carver said, "Anything will give up its secrets if you love it enough." Tend to your mind, love it, and it will gradually reveal itself to you. All the unwanted elements of your unconscious mind that stir you up and cause such anguish, when held in the embrace of love, will surface and be pacified in the warm caring light of awareness.

Holding environments

The British pediatrician and psychiatrist Donald Winnicott wrote about "holding environments," which are loving spaces created by family members, mostly parents, and that allow for the healthy development of a child. A holding environment is like an extension of the security and warmth created by the mother's womb, which is the ideal physical holding environment. It's an intuitive idea that has lifelong repercussions. Good holding environments nurture good people; bad holding environments nurture bad people. People born into violent and abusive families have a much harder time in life than those born into loving ones.

Holding environments provide a place of refuge, a "green zone" of security, that becomes the ground, and space, for growth and development. On a psychological and spiritual level, the heartfulness of meditation creates the ultimate holding environment—because we can take it with us. It's the environment of our own mind, which is not dependent on any external environment. Meditation shows us how to properly hold (but not grasp) our thoughts with love, receptivity, equanimity, and accommodation. A holding environment, in this case, nurtures a skillful relationship to whatever arises in our mind, which ironically is not about holding at all. It's about letting go.

In this regard, meditation is a kind of inner re-parenting, as psychologist Tara Bennett-Goleman refers to it. If your parents didn't instill these qualities, along with a sense of security, strength, flexibility and kindness, meditation can still do that. You can still nurture your "inner child" of meditation, and help it mature into all these noble qualities. Tara writes about the fruits of this proper relationship:

> [With meditation] we become less dependent on externals to determine our inner state as we anchor our attention in a larger awareness, one not defined by our outer condition. Our sense of calmness and an inner security grows stronger as we turn toward a nurturing awareness within, instead of depending on other people for this. Calmness can grow into equanimity during life's turbulence, which gives us a place to stand within, a nonreactive awareness, and a balanced perspective... . Enhancing our focus and clarity lets us access more of our mind's true potential. We have more room to see clearly, whether our own emotional issues or deeper insights ... Along with calm clarity comes an understanding and a sense of compassion for the suffering caused by our own—and others'—distorted mode perceptions. We can see and acknowledge the poignancy of our shared human condition. We gain a great capacity for inner attunement and a growing confidence that we can take charge of our internal worlds.[12]

In other words, we grow up.

---

12 See *Mind Whispering: A New Map to Freedom from Self-Defeating Emotional Habits*, by Tara Bennett-Goleman, HarperOne, New York, 2013.

Conclusion

Mindfulness is very simple. *Remembering* to be mindful is the hard part. A synonym for mindlessness is forgetfulness. We're good at that. In Tibetan, "mindfulness" literally means "to recollect, remember." We're not so good at that. That's where mindfulness becomes a practice: we practice remembering to come back to the present moment.

We start the practice of mindfulness-heartfulness on the meditation cushion, but the ultimate goal is to extend it to daily life. That's the magic of meditation. It naturally expands. After practicing on the cushion you may find yourself more present for everyday life. When you wash the dishes you might find that you're really washing them, and therefore doing a better job—with love. When conversing with your friend, you may find that you're listening more intently—and caring more. When you go for a walk, you're actually there for it. You feel the earth beneath your feet, the warmth of the sun on your face, and the space around you as never before. You are tending to every step.

We're not going to talk too much in this book about meditation and spirituality, simply because I want to make our journey as practical as possible. But our journey would be incomplete if we didn't touch on the spiritual aspects of meditation. If we associate spirituality with depth, then it's easy to see how meditation leads to spiritual-like experiences. By tending to the world with mindfulness-heartfulness, you may find that your ordinary experience becomes spiritual. Zen teacher Karen Maezen Miller says, "It's hard for us to believe that attention is all there is to it, and so we complicate things with our judgment—debasing the ordinary as insignificant and idealizing the spiritual as unattainable—never seeing that the two are one."

Do not let the simplicity of mindfulness fool you. It is precisely because it's so simple that it becomes so profound.

CHAPTER 3

What is Meditation—Part Two

As beautiful as the experience of mindfulness is, by itself it will not get you to the pinnacle of meditation. While mindfulness can calm the mind, only awareness can show you why it was disturbed to begin with. Without awareness meditation we will never learn how to prevent the mind from getting stirred up again. A turbulent mind remains forever superficial. A peaceful mind matures into depth.

If being totally present was the only ingredient to the deepest forms of happiness or spiritual accomplishment, then most animals would be constantly happy or even enlightened. It's impossible to say for sure, because more evolved animals like dolphins and dogs display higher brain functions, but most animals seem to be locked into the present moment. They seem to be free from distracting thoughts, but that doesn't make them truly free.

In order to reap the fruits of meditation, the second part of meditation, or awareness, is necessary. Mindfulness is slowing down and even stopping the mind. Awareness is seeing. This is the heart of meditation: stop and see. We cannot transcend (our difficult thoughts, emotions etc.) what we cannot see.

Most of the time our mind is just a buzz of activity. Thoughts are jammed together like a Los Angeles highway during rush hour. Mindfulness is like pulling over into a rest area. You step out of your car, feel the fresh air, and relax. Awareness is like checking out the views, appreciating things that were a blur just a moment ago.

When I first started meditating, the only thing I saw was an endless stream of thoughts. I never realized my mind was so cluttered. Every new thought was tailgating the one ahead of it, and squeezed by the thought behind it. There was no space in my mind. With such a busy and crowded mind no wonder I felt stressed out.

After meditating for several months my mind started to slow down. For the first time in my life I saw the gaps between my thoughts. This was a revelation, and my first experience of awareness. I could actually detect the space between my thoughts—something I had never seen before. As I continued to meditate, I saw more and more space, and with it came more and more peace. It was a breath of fresh air, like opening the window in a stuffy room.

I then noticed that the external world seemed clearer than before. It was subtle at first, but I realized I could see and hear more. I never heard birds chirping this way before. My morning coffee smelled richer, my croissant tasted sweeter. I found myself more sensitive, more awake, and more alive. Nothing had really changed out there. I was just more aware.

Mindfulness is like taking the surface of a churned up body of water and settling it down. Awareness is like looking down into the depths of that calm water and seeing things that were previously invisible. Before mindfulness meditation, thoughts and emotions keep kicking up the sand and the bottom remains forever murky. But once we stop churning things up, the waters of the mind become clear.

Sometimes when I teach meditation I'll take a small jar filled with water and some sediment and set it on my side table. You can see the dregs on the bottom, but the water is crystal clear. Without saying anything I'll shake the jar and set it back down. It's instantly muddied. But if I don't continue to jiggle it, the debris settles and everything becomes clear again. People get it: relax your mind and everything settles.

Now you can see deeper into your mind than ever before, and thoughts and emotions stand out sharply. This allows us to become familiar with them.

Contemplation - Clear or cloudy?

When you look at your mind, can you see anything but your thoughts? Is there anything visible "below" them, or is your mind so stirred up that you can't see to the "bottom"? Without some experience of settling your mind in meditation, it's impossible to see things clearly—and to get to the bottom of things. Don't get discouraged. Just realizing that your mind is murky is a big first step. Not being able to see through your thoughts can inspire you to clarify your mind, and be curious as to what lies "below."

Familiarity

Why do you want to look into the depths of your mind and heart? Because that's where real freedom and happiness lies. Freedom lies not in getting rid of thoughts and emotions, which is a common misconception, but by becoming familiar with them and discovering what lies below. The mental habits and mindlessness that cause suffering operate unconsciously and automatically. They're below the surface. That's what makes them so dangerous. What we are unconscious of we are the slaves of. Awareness meditation brings these bad habits up and onto the surface of conscious awareness, allowing us to be free of them.

Why not be satisfied with a calm or mindful mind? Because there's so much more to see. And because it's possible to get attached to meditative states, and therefore stuck in subtle traps. You can get attached to the calmness of meditation, use it as a way to escape from life, and forget that the point is not meditation. The point is *meditation in action*, or living a full life. Without awareness meditation, you may settle your mind with mindfulness, but when thoughts arise in life and you can't relate to them properly, your meditation goes out the window as fast as a thought goes through your head.

The Tibetan word for meditation is *gom*, which means "to become familiar with." Meditation cushions are called *gomdens*, or "seats of familiarity," and monasteries are called *gompas,* or "places of familiarity." Meditation is about becoming familiar with your mind and heart, with who you really are. Being present with your mind is the foundation; becoming familiar with it is the fruition. This may seem strange, since our mind is such an intimate part of ourselves. But unless we slow down and take a look, most of us are unfamiliar with our own mind. We're aware of the thoughts and emotions that *occupy* our mind, but we don't know much about mind itself, or what thoughts really are.

"Occupy," or "possess," is a good description of what thoughts do. Like an invading army that conquers and occupies a country, thoughts and emotions have the power to conquer and occupy our mind. Someone who is possessed with anger or passion, for example, has been conquered by that emotion. They even act possessed, doing things they would never do in their right mind, and that they later regret. Like a bull in a china shop, someone can be so obsessed with a thought or feeling that they're unaware, or indifferent, about what happens to others. When the spiritual traditions talk about liberation, they are referring to how meditation liberates us from these invaders.

We may not live our lives possessed or obsessed to such a degree, but every tiny thought, if we're not mindful, has the potential to take control of our mind and therefore our life. In order to free ourselves and regain control, we have to become familiar with these intruders—and relate to them properly. We can't relate to something we're not familiar with.

Proper relationship

Before we discuss proper relationship, we need to look at what is meant by an improper one. Inappropriate relationship means relating to most thoughts or emotions as if they were a big deal. If we relate to our thoughts as solid and real, that gives them an importance they don't inherently have. That's improper relationship. Our thoughts and emotions then get heavy, which drags us down. Getting all tangled up in our thoughts also keeps us up at night, ties us into knots, and causes all sorts of missteps. Because we take our thoughts and emotions so seriously, we get tossed around by those thoughts and emotions like a leaf in an autumn windstorm.

If we feel we need to express every thought or act out every emotion, that's also an improper relationship. That's what creates so much trouble with lovers, family members, or the world. It can even land us in jail. A surge of passion or aggression arises and we get carried away. We act on it. If we repress our thoughts and emotions that's also an improper relationship. As any psychologist will tell you, repression eventually causes the thought or emotion to squirt out in unhealthy ways.

Inappropriate relationship is the source of all our suffering. If we could alter our relationship and see thoughts and emotions for what they really are, we would bring peace to our mind, to others, and to the world.

Meditation shows us that we take our thoughts and emotions much too seriously. We believe them, give them power they don't naturally have, and that power comes back to control our lives.

We're suckers for the contents of our mind, and don't realize that this mind has been lying to us most of our lives. It's convinced us to act out all sorts of things. It continues to get us into heaps of trouble. Meditation shows you that you don't need to get pulled into everything you feel, and take your thoughts and emotions so personally. Getting sucked into everything sucks us out of reality and into all manner of deception, paranoia, or fantasy.

Don't get me wrong. Thoughts and emotions are obviously what make us human. We couldn't live without them. There are beautiful thoughts that blossom into great works of art, loving thoughts that benefit many, and deep emotions that are the most treasured experiences of life. These arise when we relate to thoughts and emotions properly. The problems arise when we allow our thoughts and emotions to dominate our lives. This most human quality of thinking and feeling, if related to inappropriately, can turn us into animals. A mind that is out of control leads to a life that's out of control. There's truth to the bumper sticker that says, "Don't believe everything you think."

Meditation is learning how to relate *to* your mind instead of *from* it. And that's a big difference. Until you experience meditation, and the sense of perspective it provides, the idea of relating *to* your mind may seem foreign. That's because we're always relating *from* it. A thought pops up about turning on the TV and you act from it; a feeling arises about reaching out to your friend and you act from it. There's obviously nothing wrong with turning on the TV or calling your friend, but having thoughts and emotions drive us around uncontrollably can drive us out of our mind. There *is* something wrong when a thought arises that tells you to steal a TV, or to hurt your friend, and you act from that thought. There is something off when you impulsively act on selfish thoughts.

If we train ourselves to relate *to* our mind, the same thoughts and emotions that once mastered our lives now become our servants. We're no longer slaves to whatever we think and feel. Meditation allows us to step back from a thought, to bring space to a feeling, and to make an intelligent choice. Do I really need to act on that whim? What would happen if I let that feeling evaporate? Once we see thoughts and emotions more clearly, and therefore objectively, we can then decide what to do with them. This is the wellspring of freedom.

Meditation helps us decide what to accept and what to reject in our mind, and therefore how to help or hinder ourselves and others. It gives us the chance to pause, take a closer look at each thought or emotion, and ask ourselves: if I say this, or do that, is it going to help me or anyone else? What will happen if I pursue this thought or express that emotion? We always have a choice. We can water the weeds in our mind or we can water the flowers.

I was at work the other day and caught the impulse to gossip about a co-worker. I realized that if I blurted out my mindless opinions I would only be adding to an escalating problem, and selfishly trying to get others to agree with my version of things. By pausing to bring awareness to that thought or feeling, I related to it properly and freed myself and others from verbal litter.

Meditation doesn't change anything in the outer world. It changes the way we relate to everything. In other words, thoughts and emotions still arise. The world with all its wonders and worries continues. We still think, feel, see, taste and touch. We haven't changed a thing *out there.* The revolution happens *in here.* Because we can finally see and relate to things properly, we strip them of their power to control us or scare us. It's like looking behind the curtain in the Wizard of Oz to see what's really going on behind the scenes. Or like a sturdy tree, we're no longer swayed by the winds of change or the whims of our mind. We're firmly rooted in the present moment, and the steadiness that grows from that ground.

This doesn't mean we become thoughtless and emotionless zombies, or somehow less human. Meditation doesn't whitewash the mind. It whitewashes the way we interact with it. As we'll see later, we actually hear and see and taste and feel more than ever. We become more human, more alive. But we become less fickle. Sogyal Rinpoche says:

> We often wonder what to do about negativity or certain troubling emotions. In the spaciousness of meditation, you can view your thoughts and emotions with a totally unbiased attitude. When your attitude [relationship to them] changes, then the whole atmosphere of your mind changes, even the very nature of your thoughts and emotions. When you become more agreeable, then they do; if you have no difficulty with them, they will have no difficulty with you either.[13]

Big mind

In meditation you learn to accept whatever happens, because you can accommodate it. Meditation opens the mind and makes it big. Big in terms of being spacious, not in terms of being inflated. Small minds have less room. They can get defensive or offensive. A tiny thought or irritation arises and a small mind can't relate to it. Someone else's appearance, behavior or beliefs don't fit into a small mind, and it may react aggressively or indifferently. There's too much friction. It's like being in a crowd on a hot summer day. Everything feels claustrophobic and abrasive. "I don't have room for that. I can't handle this." These are expressions of a mind unable to relate to experience. Much of our suffering comes from our inability to accommodate experience.

A big mind, however, can easily hold whatever arises. It's not moved, or polluted, by thoughts or emotions. It's open and receptive. There's plenty of room for different thoughts, and for

---

13 See *Glimpse After Glimpse, Daily Reflections on Living and Dying,* by Sogyal Rinpoche, HarperOne, New York, NY, 1995, July 2 entry.

people from all walks of life. It doesn't mean you have to agree with whatever arises, or that you shouldn't act out on what you truly think or feel. A meditative mind allows you to look at things more objectively, see them more clearly, relate to them properly, and then act intelligently.

Contemplation - Why do you drink?

*If you drink alcohol, or take mind-altering substances, why do you do so? Are you trying to soften the hard contents of your mind, making them somehow less real and therefore less painful? Are you trying to escape from your thoughts and emotions, creating some distance from them? Are you fundamentally trying to alter your **relationship** to your thoughts and emotions? Mind-altering substances are relationship-altering. Is there a healthier way to do the same thing?*

Awareness and letting go

Having a big mind comes largely from our ability to let go. You can't have a big mind if you're always grasping onto things. Grasping shrinks the mind. Letting go opens it. Letting go is a big deal in meditation—and life. Our unwillingness to let go is one reason we suffer. If you're hung up on someone or something, passively attached or actively grasping, you may suffer in direct proportion to your level of grasping. The pain of losing your favorite mug, your job, or your lover is directly related to your level of attachment. When we talk about inappropriate relationship, we're largely talking about grasping and attachment.

Proper relationship, therefore, means learning how to let go. It means learning how to love without attachment, and appreciate without grabbing. Mindfulness puts us fully in touch with things to love and appreciate. Awareness allows us to release them. This "touch-and-go" is part of the practice of mindfulness and awareness, and with it the mind gradually transforms from Velcro to Teflon, which allows suffering to slip away. The meditation master Chögyam Trungpa said:

> Having experienced the precision of mindfulness, we might ask the question of ourselves, "What should I do with that? What can I do next?" And awareness reassures us that we do not really have to do anything with it but can leave it in its own natural place. It is like discovering a beautiful flower in the jungle; shall we pick the flower and bring it home, or shall we let the flower stay in the jungle? Awareness says leave the flower in the jungle, since it is the natural place for that plant to grow. *So awareness is the willingness not to cling to the discoveries of mindfulness, and mindfulness is just precision—* things are what they are. Mindfulness is the vanguard of awareness. [emphasis added][14]

Some Asian countries use a clever trap to snare monkeys. Hunters place a banana into a small crack between some rocks. A monkey comes along, slides his hand through the crack, grabs the banana, and is unable to slide his clenched fist back through the crack. What keeps the monkey trapped? The force of his desire and attachment. He only has to release his grip to set himself free, but it's a rare ape that does that. We may not grasp bananas with the same passion as our biological ancestors, but there are many other forms of modern fruit that keep us equally stuck. Just look at how you grasp after your delicious thoughts and emotions. When Zen talks about "opening the hand of thought," this is what they're talking about.

Beginning meditators often get too tight in the technique. They think that the meditative state has to be captured and sustained. "Touch-and-go" also applies to the technique, to mindfulness itself. If you try to hold onto the present moment with rigid mindfulness, your meditation loses freshness and spontaneity. It

---

14 From *The Mindfulness Revolution: Leading Psychologists, Scientists, Artists, and Meditation Teachers on the Power of Mindfulness in Daily Life*, edited by Barry Boyce, Shambhala Publications, Boston, p 47.

can get heavy handed or stiff, and lead to resentment. Once you contact the present moment, don't hang on to it. Just touch it and go. Trungpa says, "'Go' does not mean that we have to turn our backs on the experience and shut ourselves off from it; it means just being in it without further analysis and without further reinforcement." So letting go means we also have to "open the hand of meditation" and release the present moment. Touching the present moment doesn't mean grasping after it.

The witness

Close your left eye. Take your right hand, palm facing in, and cup it over your open right eye. What do you see? Nothing. Your palm is so close to you that you can't see it. Now extend your hand to arm's length. The distance allows you to see all the lines and callouses in your palm, things that weren't visible a moment ago.

Mindfulness-awareness meditation is like that. Our thoughts and emotions are like our palm, so close to us that we can't really see them. So close that we identify with them. With meditation we step back from what occupies our mind, and allow the natural light of awareness to illuminate our thoughts and emotions. We see them in a new light, picking up details we've never seen before. Not only can we see our thoughts more clearly, we can see how they flow into each other, how they weave this way and that like the bends in a river, and how they sweep us along in different directions. We paradoxically do this not by getting closer to them, but by pulling away.

Meditation makes you aware of all these moving thoughts and emotions from an unmoving vantage point, a center of awareness that's deeper than your thoughts. This helps you separate, or distance yourself, from the often troublesome contents of your mind. As you become more familiar with this silent, spacious, and steady center, you start to identify with that, and not with all the moving parts (your fickle thoughts and emotions). Thoughts and emotions always come and go, leaving a heap of trouble in their wake. Your silent center is forever stable. As you learn to trust this center, your "observer self," you return to that and not to your thoughts, for your source of identity. You learn how to take refuge in this safe harbor of silent awareness, not the stormy seas that lie outside. It's like sailing home. You have arrived at the port of your being.

This elucidation of your innermost being is liberating. Seeing that you're not your thoughts and emotions from this new vantage point eliminates your identification with them. They no longer have power over you. You're free. Meditation shows you how to dis-identify with who you are not, for example the thought that you're worthless, incapable, or unlovable, and to identify with who you really are—this silent, spacious, and stable center of awareness.

This gives new meaning to the term "meditation center." It's both an outer physical place and an inner spiritual place. The whole purpose of an outer center is to direct you to your inner center. That's the real meditation center, and that's where you truly want to go. That's what any book, teacher, or physical center is ultimately trying to show you. Take refuge in the center of yourself, not all the distracting stuff that orbits it.

Meditation nurtures the awareness that allows you to witness things rather than being sucked into them. Instead of getting involved with everything that pops into your mind, you mentally and emotionally stand back and view things more objectively.

Sometimes when I go to a public facility I play a witness awareness game. I sit and watch everybody walk by. There are a few simple rules to this game: don't get involved with whoever walks by, and pay attention to what you feel if you do get involved. Each person represents a thought or emotion. Just like in meditation, I don't try to stop these people as they walk by, and I don't chase after them. I let them come into my field of vision and then let them walk away. At first there's a tug to fantasize and follow what I like, and to resist what I don't. But eventually I relax into this liberating witness awareness. Then it doesn't matter who walks by. Nothing hooks me. People still come and go but I'm free of them. I appreciate their brief appearances, delight in the colors and fashions they wear, but then let them go their way.

With this game, and with meditation, I have discovered that the world is full of mental and physical hooks—things and thoughts that snag me. Sometimes they drag me down, other times they lift me up. Meditation allows me to see them, and to avoid or accept their snare. In my game, if I see someone coming and get caught in watching them approach, that represents thinking about the future. I notice I've been caught, and let that thought of the future go. If I follow someone else as they pass by, that represents thinking about the past. Once again, I just notice the hook and let it go. If I hold my gaze gently but firmly in front of me, that represents staying in the present. This is how I win in meditation, and in life. As they say in many lotteries—"you must be present to win."

Mind diving

Last year I learned how to scuba dive. I trained in a swimming pool, and then did my first open water dive in Cozumel, Mexico. I was really nervous before the open dive. We were a mile from shore with waves big enough to put me on edge, and five miles from the nearest dock. I jumped into the ocean with my instructor and immediately inflated my buoyancy control vest to stay afloat. We had to wait a few minutes for the other divers to join us, long enough to amplify my anxiety as the surface chop tossed me around. Even though I had my mask on, water was still splashing into my face as I struggled to stay balanced. When we were finally ready, the instructor signaled that it was time to release the air from our vests and go down. My heart was pounding with a mixture of anticipation and fear.

The minute I dropped below the waves a spectacular new world unfolded before me. I looked down and saw a mind-bending vista of coral and fish I had never seen before, with everything shimmering in the turquois light of the Caribbean. I longed to explore this new terrain of unfamiliar life forms, dazzling colors, and fascinating new shapes. Off to one side, the coral dropped into a deep and dark abyss that sent a chill up my spine. Too deep, too scary. Maybe later. I looked up to the surface and noticed the boat bobbing to and fro, sunlight glistening off the hull. But what struck me the most was the extraordinary stillness, silence, and vast sense of freedom and space. The contrast from the unsettling surface chop to deep peace and quiet was dramatic.

I was suddenly liberated. The waves were still up there thrashing about, but I was below them. They no longer had any effect on me. Instead of splashing me in the face and tossing me around, I was able to see them in a peaceful new light. I also felt weightless, like I was floating in outer space. The result of these sensations was a sense of utter delight. For the next forty minutes I played in the deep water like a carefree child.

This is a beautiful analogy for meditation. Before we engage in meditation, we're stuck living on the surface of life, and the shallows of our mind. There's not much depth. We're swept away by the mere appearance of things, and out of touch with their deeper essence. The currents of our thoughts, and the tidal waves of our emotions, throw us about like Styrofoam on the ocean. Life splashes into our face and stings our eyes. A thought pops up and we feel we must act on it. A wave of emotion comes up and we're moved to indulge it. Everything is moving all over the place and we're moving with it.

If we're living on the surface, we tend to be impulsive, unsettled, and uneasy. We don't even realize there's an option, another way to be. The phrase "surface of our mind" has no meaning. Surface as opposed to what? What else is there except our thoughts and emotions? But the instant we drop below this surface chop and into the stillness of our deeper mind, a new world opens up.

Meditation is like "mind diving." It introduces you to a world that has always been there, but that you've never experienced before. This deeper mind is a breathtaking world of new life forms—wondrous and infinitely vast. It's an introduction to your deeper self.

You may feel like you have to go really deep to experience this wonder, and that meditation is for people specially equipped to go to these depths. But just like any form of diving, you only have to drop below the surface a little bit to discover a fantastic new world. All of us, not matter how restless and active our minds are, can take this dive. You only have to descend below your thoughts and emotions a tiny amount to "look up" and see them in a new light. Meditation shows you how to dip into the silence and stillness that lies below all mental activity.

The difference between a beginner and a seasoned meditator is that the veteran is more familiar, and comfortable, at deeper levels. They can go deeper, stay down longer, and therefore see more. And they can connect to this depth more quickly, and frequently, in the hubbub of daily life. But the magic begins the minute you submerge.

Beginning meditators are still infatuated with the surface of things. This is because they're so familiar, and therefore comfortable, with the outer aspects of mind and life. Even though they've seen below the surface, which represents the mere appearance of thoughts and emotions, they still enjoy the chop. In other words, even though they have tasted freedom, which is the deeper reality that lies beneath the mere appearance of thoughts and emotions, they're still attached to the entertainment that thoughts provide. Thoughts and emotions may torment us, but they also provide welcome distraction.

The more you dive into the depths of your mind the less interested you become in surface distractions. All the dramas of thought and emotion pale in comparison to the beauty of your deeper mind and the profundity of the inner world. Outer appearances seem increasingly "thin." It's just froth.

As a meditator progresses into the depths of their mind, going deeper and staying down longer, they become less involved with worldly silliness. They see it, but they're not interested. They see through the folly of mere appearance. The inner world is so much richer. Superficial thoughts and emotions still arise—you still think and feel as needed to function in the world—but you're no longer swayed by the waves. The Styrofoam mind turns into meteoric iron. You cut through appearances and drop into reality.

My scuba experience was so powerful that I sometimes use that feeling of descent in my meditation. When my mind is tossed around with thoughts, I'll flash on that feeling of dropping beneath the surface. Within a few moments I'm below it all, "looking up" at my thoughts. They're still up there making a mess, but I'm not.

I'll also do this if I wake up in the middle of the night and can't go back to sleep. That's what's so great about meditation. Once you get the basics you can apply it to anything. That's the whole point. My insomnia, like my thought-filled mind, is no longer a problem. The difficult experiences of my life are less of a problem. I also like this diving image because it's aligned with the humble spirit of meditation. I'm not above it all—I'm beneath it.

But staying down forever is not the point. Meditation is not the final point. The point is to gain access to the depths of your mind, see through the surface silliness, then come back up and live in the world with this new perspective. Everything still arises on the surface of life, but now you know better. You're no longer fooled.

Conclusion

These last few chapters have given us a good working definition of meditation. Your practice and study will continue to refine it. It's a lifelong endeavor. Meditation is as vast and deep as the ocean, and we've just skimmed the surface. But this is enough to get us started, and to help us take the plunge. Sogyal Rinpoche says:

> To meditate is to make a complete break with how we "normally" operate, for it is a state free of all cares and concerns, in which there is no competition, no desire to possess or grasp at anything, no intense and anxious struggle, and no hunger to achieve: an ambitionless state where there is neither acceptance nor rejection, neither hope nor fear, a state in which we slowly begin to release all those emotions and concepts that have imprisoned us into the space of natural simplicity.[15]

---

15 See *Glimpse After Glimpse, Daily Reflections on Living and Dying,* by Sogyal Rinpoche, HarperOne, New York, NY, 1995, May 11 entry.

CHAPTER 4

What Meditation is Not

While it's important to understand what meditation is, it's just as important to understand what it is not. There are so many misconceptions. The reason some people are uneasy or even afraid of meditation is because they don't understand it. If we don't know about something, we tend to project our assumptions, prejudices, and biases onto it. For example, if we don't know about Islam, we may take the behavior of a few bad people and project it onto all Muslims. It's a human tendency to pigeonhole things, and to fear those who are different.

Because meditation may be foreign, it's easy to plaster it with our hopes and fears. Some people hope that meditation will cure everything. Others fear it will make them crazy. I've heard an amazing variety of definitions, from the humorous (meditation leads to "tantric sex"), to the incredible (meditation will show me how to levitate), to the absurd (meditation is evil, unleashing the devil within). For some, meditation is a mystical religion. For others it's a New Age fad.

The technique of meditation is so simple that it's hard to believe. A common reaction when instruction is given is for people to say, "That's it? There has to be more to it than this!" So they add more, which distorts the simplicity of the practice. They forget that the profundity comes from the simplicity.

Not about getting rid of thoughts

Perhaps the most common misunderstanding is that meditation means getting rid of thoughts. Many beginners feel that thoughts are bad, and must be eliminated in order to have good meditation. They imagine meditation as a blank state of mind, devoid of thought or emotion. In over twenty years as a meditation instructor, this is the single greatest source of frustration and discouragement. "I'm a horrible meditator, I just can't stop thinking." "If only I could stop my thoughts, then I would be able to meditate." "I knew I couldn't meditate, I can't control my mind." We then try to spank our thoughts out of existence and end up spanking ourselves. We get hard on ourselves and give up.

This kind of thinking is what Alcoholics Anonymous calls "stinkin' thinkin'." Don't stink up your meditation with these thoughts. Meditation is not about getting rid of your thoughts. It's about becoming familiar with them, and then establishing a healthy relationship to them. This distinction cannot be over-emphasized. Thoughts are not a problem. Thinking is just what the mind does. Thoughts will always be part of your mind, just as waves are part of the ocean. You might slow thoughts down or stop them temporarily, but you'll never be able to force thoughts out of your mind forever. Trying to do so will only make you miserable.

Thoughts only become a problem if we feed them with our attention, or let them distract us from the richness of the present moment. It's natural for thoughts to pop up in our mind, but unnatural to let them occupy our mind. Thoughts have a pattern of stringing together, one thought leads to the next thought, then the next one. This is mindlessness, or a runaway mind. Instead of indulging or suppressing thoughts and emotions, the point is to view them with acceptance and openness.

Thoughts are like chatter. In meditation, just don't listen to them. Let them chat away, but don't pay attention to them. How to deal with thoughts in meditation will be discussed in detail when we describe the technique in Chapter Eight.

Meditation is about making more friends, not more enemies. If we feel that thoughts are bad, they become the enemy and our mind becomes a battleground. We end up fighting with ourselves in a war that we'll always lose. The mind has an endless supply of thoughts to send to the front lines of consciousness, and you'll never keep them out or beat them away. The point is to love your mind, just the way it is, and not try to defeat it.

I occasionally have insomnia, which used to drive me crazy. I would wake up in the middle of the night and tie myself into knots trying to force myself back to sleep. Trying to get rid of my thoughts only made it worse. The more I tried, the more they seemed to multiply. One night, out of desperation, I replaced my fighting attitude with a loving one. Instead of boxing with my thoughts I began hugging them. I starting saying to myself, almost like a mantra: "love your mind, love your mind." It worked! I gradually relaxed and dropped back into sleep. Being kind to your thoughts, to yourself, also works with meditation.

If you can relate to your thoughts the way a caring parent relates to their child, you will understand the heart of meditation. Thoughts are the children of your mind. Relate to them with unconditional love. Our thoughts, like our kids, manifest in countless ways. Sweet in one second, nasty in the next. But if we embrace them just as they are, we can remove a great deal of unnecessary stress—in meditation or life.

We can handle our children's behavior because we're familiar with them, and because we care. We know the tantrum won't last, the pouting spell will evaporate, and the rebellious attitude is temporary. We realize that there's more to their behavior than meets the stranger's eye. We love them no matter what because they're a natural part of us. At the same time, we don't get swept up in their actions. We look deeper into their goodness, and let the outbursts dissolve on their own. Unless you're emotionally disturbed, you don't think about killing your kids or locking them away. Because you know them you know how to relate to them.

As with your children so with your mind. As we discussed, meditation is a form of inner re-parenting. Accept your thoughts without indulging or spanking them. Get to know them, but never try to get rid of them. If you're ever in doubt about what to do, in meditation or life, default into acceptance and love.

Not about creating a special state of mind

Many people feel that meditation is about creating a special or "spiritual" state of mind. This is a misconception similar to the last, and just as damaging. We see pictures of "holy people" in serene meditation, or imagine meditators absorbed in thought-free states. If it's not bliss, or a vacant mind, then it must be some other version of what we deem meditation to be.

This is where we get into a slippery area of meditation. While meditation is similar to other things in life, it's also unique. There are aspects of meditation that are unlike anything else. Until we actually experience them, we tend to misunderstand them. There are questions about meditation that have a simple yes *or* no answer, and others that require a more complex yes *and* no response. The question of whether meditation creates a special state of mind falls into the yes *and* no category.

Let's deal with the "yes" part first. It's reasonable to think that meditation brings about special states. If it didn't, why bother? If meditation doesn't make me feel better, I'd rather go to the movies. The tricky point is that while meditation does result in peaceful and even ecstatic states, if we try to develop these experiences directly, or with too much ambition, we ironically short-circuit the process. It's like trying to hold onto a drop of mercury. If you try to pin it down, it squirts out the side.

Remember that the magic of meditation comes from relaxation. If you try too hard to relax you won't relax. But if you don't try at all you won't be meditating. The idea here is that the way to achieve exalted states of meditation is not to try to. Or at least not try too hard. Special experiences happen when we simply relax. Don't try for the fireworks and you may see them.

The secret, therefore, is to accept and embrace yourself *just as you are*. That's when the magic happens. Don't try to be the Dalai Lama. Be yourself, and you may find you're starting to manifest qualities like the Dalai Lama. Don't try to be Jesus Christ. Be yourself, and you may discover your Christ-like qualities.

Sometimes it's taught that striving in meditation is the only obstacle. You will attain special states by not trying to be special. This is how meditation is unlike most things: you largely achieve it by *not* doing.

Meditation is ordinary. So much so that it's extraordinary. It's not designed to rocket you into heavenly realms of experience. It's designed to plant you firmly on the ground. Real meditation redefines "spiritual." It helps you discover the most spiritual states in the most common events. Folding your laundry or taking out the trash becomes spiritual if you're fully present for it.

So the "no" part is that meditation is not about creating special states of mind, at least in the way we usually define "special." It's about accepting any state of mind—any experience—and discovering that *that* is what's special.

Not about self-improvement

This is another tricky one, because meditation does improve things. Your life does get better. But self-improvement strategies per se are not about acceptance. Most of them are based on the overt or covert message that there's something wrong with you, and you need to get better. They're subtly aggressive. The miracle, and near paradox, of meditation is that you will improve if you learn how to accept yourself just the way you are. It's almost like a Zen koan, or spiritual riddle. Let yourself be, and you will become better.

It's more accurate to say that meditation is about life-improvement. As you become more fully present for your life, it gets richer, fuller, more satisfying. You'll find yourself more alive and awake, and that's an improvement. But even here it depends on how you define "improvement." If you think meditation will make you feel good all the time, you'll be disappointed. Meditation is not a narcotic. It's about awareness. You just feel *everything* more.

It's strange from a non-meditative perspective, but even feeling bad more fully feels better, because it feels genuine. The experience is more complete and therefore fulfilling—no matter how bad it seems. There's nothing wrong with feeling bad. It's an honest part of life. Trying to feel good all the time is dishonest, because it's not in harmony with the way the world works. Meditation is not about making you feel good all the time. It's about making you feel real. And oddly enough, at a much deeper level, that feels "good." It's the goodness that comes from truth, no matter how rugged that truth may be. It's good to know the truth about anything, even if that doesn't always feel good. So meditation improves things the way truth improves things.

One of the sneakiest obstacles in meditation is a deeply entrenched desire to feel a particular way. Many meditators think that if they just practice hard enough they'll feel better. That's true, but again it depends on how you define "better." Meditation is not about feeling *any* particular way. It's about developing the ability to touch into, and therefore feel without preference, whatever arises. Stay open to whatever you experience. Don't close down and strive for a particular experience.

Meditation eventually shows you that you are perfect just the way you are—with all your thoughts and emotions. This is a breathtaking discovery, and so hard for most of us to believe. For me it was a tremendous sigh of relief, perhaps the greatest benefit of meditation in my life. I'm no longer driven to be good in order to be loved, as I spoke about in the introduction. I've learned to love myself—to be myself—and find that most people love me for that. While I still have a long way to go to stabilize this discovery, I know in my bones that I'm okay. The sage Sri Nisargadatta said that the essence of the meditative path is to "Make love of yourself perfect."

This is where meditation gets spiritual, because shedding all these burdens about self-improvement is part of getting en-lightened. Meditation lightens the load. As you learn how to let go of your thoughts and emotions, you learn how to drop the baggage you've been carrying around that something is wrong with you.

Not about escaping

Because life is hard, many people meditate because they want a way out. We may have images of meditators sitting peacefully on mountains, or in the silence of a monastery, and fantasize about being like that. But meditation is not about escaping from reality. It's about entering it fully. It's not about zoning out. It's about zoning in. The only thing a meditator escapes from is distraction. We retreat onto our meditation cushion not to run away from ourselves, but to face ourselves and our lives directly. With so much distraction and busyness, it can be difficult to slow down, look within, and make friends with ourselves. Endless obligations and temptations seduce us into the world and out of ourselves. When we retreat into meditation this is the only thing we retreat from.

Meditation is sometimes referred to as a warrior's path. This may seem like a strong term, but it's used because it takes courage to sit with your mind. It takes guts to simply be, and to go against the grain of entertainment and distraction. We're often human "doings," not human beings. Always on the go, endlessly doing things. Sometimes when people ask me what we do at our meditation center, I'll say "We do nothing. But we do it very well."

Meditators are peaceful warriors brave enough to stop and be. Daring enough look at themselves, and to live fearlessly in the present moment. That's where true freedom lies. When we drift off into the future or the past, we may feel like we're roaming freely, but this freedom is the most subtle of traps. In other words, mindlessness is actually our attempt to escape. But it never works. You might find a temporary exit in fleeting fantasies, but sooner or later you have to come back to earth.

We're constantly trying to run away from ourselves, into entertainment, alcohol, unhealthy relationships, drugs, or other infinite forms of distraction. With meditation we realize that while these activities may temporarily release our anxieties, they ultimately fall short in bringing us what we really want—which is the full experience of life as it happens *now*.

Contemplation - What do you really want?

Without honest reflection many of us don't know. We often want what others want for us, either our immediate family and friends, or even advertisers. The psychologist Eric Fromm says, "[M]an lives under the illusion that he knows what he wants, while he actually wants what he is supposed to want. In order to accept this it is necessary to realize that to know what one really wants is not comparatively easy, as most people think, but one of the most difficult problems any human being has to solve." We may feel that we want out, but maybe what we really want is a way in. Perhaps what we really want is a way to enter into the full experience of life, not run away from it.

When I did my first month-long retreat, I craved for the end of the day. I longed to plop into bed and indulge my thoughts. After disciplining my mind all day, I let it run wild at night. I felt like a rebellious child and I loved it! I soon realized how much I used this time as an escape. Each night was like running off to the movies, and the nearest theater was right here in my mind.

This sharp contrast, between the work of being mindful all day and the flagrant release into mindlessness at night, showed me how often I use thoughts as the great escape. I only have to indulge a single thought to run away from myself or the drudgery of daily life. This is why the entertainment business is such a success. Mindlessness sells. The entertainment industry is just an extension of what we do throughout the day to escape from the abrasive aspects of reality.

There's nothing inherently wrong with entertainment. I love a good movie or novel as much as anybody. But if you're always at the movies, internal or external, who's living your life?

I was reading the Denver Post this morning and the organization of the paper struck me. The first section is about international news, mostly the calamity around the world. The second section is about local news, the distress in my city and state. There's the occasional uplifting article, but most of it's depressing. Then the third and fourth sections, on sports and entertainment, are about how to escape from the harsh reality of the first two sections!

We're always looking for a way out. Trungpa Rinpoche said that there is no way out. The magic is to discover that there is a way in. Meditation is the way in.

Not about mind control

Mind control is another yes *and* no issue. Meditation is not about mind control in the sense of subduing what happens in your mind. If you try to control yourself in this muscular sense you'll drive yourself nuts. Meditation never forces anything. But at the same time, as we've seen, you don't just let your mind run wild. Meditation involves effort. What we do try to control is our relationship to thoughts and emotions. Sogyal Rinpoche writes:

> Take care not to impose anything on the mind. When you meditate, there should be no effort to control, and no attempt to be peaceful. Don't be overly solemn or feel that you are taking part in some special ritual; let go even of the idea that you are meditating. Let your body remain as it is, and your breath as you find it. Think of yourself as the sky, holding the whole universe.[16]

The Zen master Suzuki Roshi said that if you want to control a herd of cows you don't try to squeeze them into a corral. You give them an open pasture. Meditation controls the mind this way. You don't shut it down. You open it up. You control the mind with space, and awareness provides that space.

So the "no" part is that we don't try to control whatever happens in our mind. Let whatever happens happen. The "yes" part is that we work to control our reactions to that arising.

---

16 See *Glimpse After Glimpse, Daily Reflections on Living and Dying*, by Sogyal Rinpoche, HarperOne, New York, NY, 1995, June 10 entry.

Mindfulness is not about keeping yourself in check. It's not about scrutinizing your mind and pouncing on anything that pops up. This misunderstanding creates a critical attitude instead of an embracing one. Instead of relaxing, people get self-conscious, serious, and stiff. Mindfulness is about being precise, but that precision is gentle. Accomplished meditators have a subtle smile on their face, not a frown.

Not about concentration

Some people feel that mindfulness means thinking hard about something. While meditation does involve focus, it's not the same as concentration. Concentration scares people from meditation. Having to sit and concentrate for twenty minutes or more is intimidating. "I can't concentrate that long!" From a meditative perspective, pure concentration is too tight. Remember that meditation is about relaxation. You're not forcing your mind into the present moment. You're inviting it there.

At the same time, just hanging out is too loose. You might stay out of trouble by sitting and daydreaming, but you'll also stay out of the real practice of meditation. You do have to apply the technique.

If we relate to concentration in the truest sense of the word, "to center with," then we can talk about meditation as concentration. Meditation gathers the mind and centers it onto the moment. To get a feel for this, try this simple movement. Close your eyes and feel into your body. Slowly stretch your hands out to your sides, and then gradually raise them above your head until your palms meet. With your hands in this kind of prayer posture, slowly drop them until they come to rest at your heart. Notice the feeling. This is called the "gathering the mind" gesture. It feels good. This is the kind of concentration that meditation evokes.

Meditation is not religion

While there are many religious and spiritual traditions that use meditation, meditation itself is not religious, or even spiritual. You could say it is secular, which refers to things that are not religious, spiritual, or sacred, but even that's not accurate. Meditation is about taming and then training the mind, and nobody has a patent on that. Your mind is free of any cultural, religious, spiritual, or even scientific trappings. It's just the mind, and everybody has one. Locking meditation to any tradition is like locking exercise to one tradition. Anybody who has a body can exercise it. Anybody who has a mind can tame it. Doing pushups or going for a run is not Hindu nor Buddhist, and neither is bringing your mind back to the present moment.

The problem is one of historical association, and then conflation, which means inappropriately joining two things together. Because we see so many spiritual and religious traditions using meditation, it's easy to think that meditation therefore has to be religious. For many people, meditation is almost synonymous with Buddhism, Hinduism, or mysticism. But once you try meditation and understand it, you quickly discover it's free of any "ism." Meditation is just a tool. It's like a microscope or telescope. Anybody can sit down (mindfulness) and look (awareness) through a microscope.

You could say that meditation is religious in the sense that it cultivates noble qualities of the mind and heart, like any good religion. But philosophy or psychology can also do that. Meditation can also be "religious" in the truest sense of that word: to "link, or tie" (ligare) "back" (re). Meditation, as re-ligion, links you back to the present moment.

You could say that meditation is spiritual in the sense that it shows you there's more to life than meets the eye, and that there's something more meaningful than material things. It's also "spiritual" in the truest sense of that word. "Spirit" comes from the word "breath," which is a main object of focus in many meditations.

You could also say that meditation is scientific, in the sense that it works with direct experience. Meditation, like science, is involved in discovering what's real. They both penetrate through the superficial appearance of things, and try to get to the truth. Both require honesty. Like science, meditation also has an empirical method, and similar to science it's something you do. Both lead to genuine "scientific" (rigorous and replicable) discoveries.

You could also argue that meditation is psychological, in the sense that it works with the psyche. Like psychology, it can help us learn about our deeper selves, and resolve emotional and behavioral issues. ("Psyche" started out by meaning "breath," and developed semantically to denote "soul, spirit.")

You could even argue that meditation is a philosophy, a way of looking at mind and reality, and a way to cultivate "loving wisdom:" "philos" (loving) "sophos" (wise). Like philosophy, meditation can guide and inform an entire life.

Meditation is easily associated with all of these things, but it's simultaneously none of them. It can be used, and therefore associated, with any tradition, discipline, institution or person that deals with the mind and heart. But don't confuse the container for the content. Just because the container of religion, for example, uses meditation, doesn't mean that meditation is religion. Meditation is much bigger than that.

CHAPTER 5

How Do I Get Started?

You don't need much to get started with meditation. Whatever you do in life, wherever you are, you can start right there. On one level you only need your mind. It's like running. On one level you only need your feet. But props like shoes and socks help. Stretching before and after helps. Once you learn the basics, you can practice meditation anywhere and anytime. That's the point. Meditation isn't just what you do on your cushion. If you elect to cultivate it, it becomes a way of life. To get you going, a few tips can help. You can increase your enjoyment, and heighten the benefits of meditation, by learning some preliminary points.

Just like any new venture, getting into meditation can be initially daunting. The first time I got meditation instruction I was nervous. I didn't know what to expect. That was forty years ago, when meditation was barely mentioned in the West. I was a stranger in a strange land, afraid of what I might find in my mind, and worried that I just couldn't do it. Maybe meditation wasn't for me.

Anxiety and fear are virtually synonymous with the unknown. We're afraid of what we don't know. Even after meditating for a year, it took me awhile to commit to a meditation instructor, and even longer to finally go to a meditation center. I didn't want to join a cult and I didn't want anybody to brainwash me. In retrospect my anxiety was silly. Nothing could be more gentle than meditation.

With this said, take your time. Do what feels right. Read some books, talk to people who meditate, or take a class. If you're sampling meditation, always remember that the sample you try may not be the best for you. You could stumble onto a book written by a quack, or take a class from a charlatan. As meditation becomes more popular it also becomes more profitable. While rare, there are meditation "masters" more interested in emptying out your wallet than in waking up your wisdom.

I learned this the hard way. On my second trip to Nepal about fifteen years ago, I was befriended by a Buddhist monk. This was at a time when I was still bewitched by anyone wearing robes. If you were wearing robes you had to be holy. I didn't know much about Buddhism, but he seemed to be saying the right things. He talked about compassion, about the path of the Buddha, and meditation. He was friendly, I was eager, so we talked for hours. At the end of our wonderful afternoon he started talking about how his monastery needed funding for some religious statues. He gave a heartfelt presentation about how poor his monastery was, and how important these statues were for all the monks. After setting up a meeting for the next day to talk more about Buddhism, I gave him two hundred dollars for the statue fund. It was the last I saw of him, and my money.

Do your homework, and realize that healthy skepticism is good. But remember that without taking a leap you'll never change. Meditation is safe. Meditation "masters" or instructors are a different matter. The vast majority are noble people, and often teach meditation for free. But just like with anything, there are fakes. Ask around. If you're considering a teacher, talk to their students, and don't be afraid to ask tough questions. Trust your intuition. I'll talk later about problems and pitfalls on the meditative path and how to avoid them.

Meditation itself is the practice of kindness. You need a really screwy understanding, and an even screwier practice, to ever hurt yourself. If it's done properly there's no way meditation can hurt you. It might ding your ego, but that's a good thing. Meditation may not always be easy, but it is harmless. And remember: nothing worthwhile is ever easy.

Attitude

The best attitude is to have a beginner's mind. This means an open mind, one that is willing to drop expectations and prejudices, and that provides the space to try something new. More often than not, meditation isn't what you initially think it is. If you approach it with too many preconceptions you'll pigeonhole meditation into one of your conceptual boxes. It either won't fit your biased view, or something will get left out. You won't get it.

Let meditation touch you on its terms, not yours. If you approach it with too many hopes, or an excessively critical mind, you will distort meditation and it will fail. Expectation is premeditated disappointment, cynicism is prearranged collapse. An attitude of "I knew it wouldn't work" or "I knew I couldn't do it" is usually a self-fulfilling prophecy. Give yourself a chance.

But at the same time, don't be naïve. Trust your intelligence and your intuition. Don't blindly accept everything you hear, which is how people get into trouble with anything. Don't be afraid to challenge a teaching or a teacher. As I said in the introduction, test meditation against your own experience. If it works for you, that's great. If it doesn't, toss it out the door.

Meditation is like science. A good scientist asks the right questions, gathers what they need, then goes to the lab and does the experiment. They don't do the experiment expecting it to fail, or with sloppy preparation. They do it honestly and openly. Then they let the results speak for themselves. If they're doing good science they don't expect anything. They just do the experiment and watch what happens. That's the best attitude. A good scientist has dedication, perseverance, curiosity, integrity, and the desire to explore and learn. Add some humor and these are also the qualities of a good meditator.

While meditation is unique, in many ways it's just like any other discipline. If you want to get good at playing the piano, or golf, or meditation, you need to do it. If you dabble at it you'll get dabbling results. You'll get out of it what you put into it.

Instruction

You can learn enough about meditation from a book to get you going, but it helps to have personal instruction. Can you really learn to play the piano from a book? Would your tennis or golf improve with a lesson? There are many nuances that only an instructor can offer. While the basic meditation instruction is standard, there are countless variations that can make the practice more workable and enjoyable. And while everyone shares the same basic qualities of mind, like attention, everybody is different. We all walk the meditative path our own way.

The point at which you might want a meditation instructor (MI) varies from person to person. Some would benefit right away, others after they've tried it awhile. Just like any discipline, it's ideal to get personal instruction from the start, but it's not mandatory. There is plenty to try out and explore on your own. Sooner or later questions will arise that only an instructor can answer. If you don't share you experience with someone more knowledgeable, it's easy to stray, get discouraged, or kid yourself. Self-deception is rampant among meditators. You think you're getting somewhere, only to find out you've been wasting your time.

The desire for personal instruction usually develops naturally. At some point you want to share your experience or refine your understanding with someone more experienced. You want to communicate your excitement or frustration. In my twenty years as a MI, people usually start out with plenty of questions and need to talk every few weeks. After awhile they get the hang of it and the need for personal guidance decreases. From every week, to every month, to maybe a few times a year.

With enough experience you become your own MI. You've got it, and you're honest with yourself. Even at that stage it helps to meet with an instructor every year or so, to make sure you're still on track. The basics are simple, but the discoveries extend throughout your life. If you don't live near a meditation instructor, you can find one to talk to via phone or Skype. Appendix Three provides a list of meditation centers that can introduce you to a MI.[17]

A meditation instructor is a blend of teacher, elder, friend, and even therapist. They are there to support you, advise you, and correct you. Conversations are always confidential. If they're not, you should find another MI. While MI's don't really do therapy, it's a fine line. Things may come up in meditation that are best handled by a therapist, and a good MI will realize that. Psychological baggage coming up in your meditation is a good thing, a topic we'll return to in the chapter "Frequently asked questions."

---

17 Eva Hudlicka, a computer scientist specializing in affective computing, a discipline where psychology, cognitive science, and computer science merge, has created a virtual interactive character, Coach Chris, to help new meditators. Hudlicka's aspiration is to develop new technology that improves access to meditation instruction, and supports practice. This is certainly just the first of many such innovations. See: www.aaai. org/ocs/index.php/SSS/SSS11/paper/viewFile/2441/2862

Your relationship with your MI can turn into a friendship, and naturally extend beyond formal instruction sessions. However, if you don't have a good feeling about your MI, either talk to them about it or find another one. A good MI will not be offended if a student chooses a different instructor. Sometimes the chemistry just isn't there. Like with any discipline, there are good instructors and bad ones. They're human. Most instructors have official training, and even testing. Ask about that. Ask them how long they've been meditating or instructing. Openness and honesty are keys to a good relationship. There are no licensing requirements, so it pays to ask questions.

Because of the psychological and even spiritual intimacy, it's possible for the desire for physical intimacy to arise with your MI. This should be addressed openly. If a MI makes unwanted advances, that's a deal-breaker. It's a violation of their spoken or unspoken contract. It's rare but it does happen. Power plays and ego trips can happen anywhere. If the MI is from a meditation center, let the director of that center know of this breach. If there's mutual attraction, then the student-teacher relationship needs to change. The student should be referred to another instructor for formal meditation instruction. This doesn't mean you can't continue to talk about meditation as a couple. It means the official role of the MI is over. It's not as restricted as the relationship with a therapist, but the MI should manifest honesty and integrity. They are there to serve you—not themselves.

Props

Meditation is a bare-bones enterprise. The only prop you really need is intention. But some outside props help. Some beginners like a more austere approach. Just give me the technique. Others want all sorts of aids. I tend to be conservative, and suggest people start out slowly, with minimal external supports. If meditation clicks with you, then gradually add whatever helps you maintain your practice.

Some investment also shows your level of commitment and can help you stick with it. But if you're resistant to any expense, you can practice meditation without buying a thing. You just need a place to sit. If you're sitting cross-legged on the floor, you can sit on some firm pillows, or even use the bottom step on a staircase. The "middle way" approach applies to many aspects of meditation. In this instance you don't want to sit on something too hard or too soft. If it's too hard your butt and back will start to hurt. If it's too soft you'll tend to slouch or get drowsy.

I recommend investing in a meditation cushion and a pad that's placed under the cushion. They're not expensive and help with proper posture. If it works for you, creating a special place for meditation is helpful. Some people like to meditate in bed. There's nothing inherently wrong with that, but we associate beds with sleeping. Sometimes I meditate in the middle of the night sitting up in my bed. It often helps me fall back asleep. Generally speaking, beds fall into the "too soft" category.

You can designate a corner of a room, or an entire room, as your meditation space. Shoji screens are inexpensive and work well to frame off a space. They also impart an oriental feeling, which is often associated with meditation. When I first started meditating as a poor undergraduate living with roommates, I cleaned out my closet and put my cushion there. It worked beautifully. I was shy about telling anybody about my practice, and only several months later caught the humor that I was literally a closet meditator.

You can also set up a small shrine or altar. This can be as simple as a box with special objects placed on it. The objective is to create a space set apart, something that inspires you, and reminds you of whatever is sacred to you. You can put some candles (which symbolizes the light of awareness), photographs of special people, or objects that have meaning. We feel the power of sacred places, like cathedrals, temples, or monasteries. The idea is to replicate that feeling in your home. There's a different feeling when you walk into a bar, a library, a clinic, or a temple. In terms of meditation, it's easy to create a space that supports you.

Since I've been meditating for so long I have a shrine room in my house. It's my most important room. Over the years I've collected special items to put into this space. I have nice brocade on my shrine, offering bowls, a few small statues, and candles. On the walls I've placed photographs of teachers, and spiritual paintings. In front of my meditation cushion I have a small table for incense, and more photographs of people who inspire me. I also have a small meditation gong, a rosary (mala) for counting mantras, and a few other Buddhist related things. Over the years I've collected photographs of loved ones who have died, and placed them on this table. The pile keeps getting bigger. It's a powerful reminder of impermanence and helps me stay on track. My meditation room is a mix of traditional and personal items that have meaning to me.

When I get lazy, or feel too tired to meditate, it's almost as if my shrine room calls for me. It's a wonderful tug back into practice. Because so much of the world is mindless, it's so easy to be dragged away from mindfulness. We forget. A space for meditation is a reminder. So much of the world takes us down, meditation props lift us up. Appendix Three lists places where you can get some props.

Intangible props

Setting aside a regular time and place for meditation is an intangible prop. The idea is to use the power of habit in your favor. Habit and routine are important when it comes to meditation. One of the challenges with meditation, or any new discipline, is establishing enough momentum to keep you going. Do anything enough and it starts to do you. The practice becomes part of your life.

It's like flossing your teeth. You know it's good for you, but unless you force yourself to do it every day at first, you just won't do it. If you muster the discipline to floss every night for a few months, you'll get to the point where it doesn't feel right if you don't floss. That's where you want to get. Give the ball a sustained push and it will roll for a long time on its own. If you stop for too long the ball stops. Then you have to crank it up again. This is where many people get discouraged and give up.

Because I've developed so much momentum by meditating all these years, it carries me. Every time I meditate I add more momentum. It just keeps rolling and I roll with it. It gets easier. As I discussed, most of the effort comes at the beginning.

Most people find meditating first thing in the morning to be the best. The day hasn't gotten away from you yet, and the mind tends to be fresh. You can practice at any time, but after a long day it's easy to cave in to fatigue. Many people would rather drink a glass of wine and watch a movie. Studies have also shown that willpower wanes as the day goes on.[18] It gets spent. So meditation in the evening is often harder for many. Whatever time you choose, stick to it. The repetition and regularity builds on itself. It's like water flowing over sandstone. If water flows over the same spot repeatedly it cuts a groove. After awhile you can't help yourself. You've fallen into the healthy habit of daily meditation, and it starts to do you.

This doesn't mean you have to tough it out and force yourself to meditate every day. That's being too tight, like a saddle that's too constricted. The horse will buck to get it off. If you're too tight, you might come to resent the practice and quit. Skipping

---

18 See *The Power of Habit: Why We Do What We Do in Life and Business,* by Charles Duhigg, Random House, New York, NY, 2012.

a day or two is okay. Giving yourself a break is okay. But I have found that being a bit tight at first is good. If you err on the side of being too loose it's easy for your meditation practice to evaporate. Before you know it it's been weeks and you just don't feel like meditating anymore. It's important to practice even on days you don't feel like it. If you only practice when you want to, you will only discover the part of you that wants to sit. Find a healthy balance, but remember that it is a *practice*. As they say in many advertisements, "some assembly (effort) required."

Finding like-minded people to support you is invaluable. Even though meditation is getting more popular, most of the world doesn't meditate. That means there's peer pressure that can keep you from meditation. Your friends and colleagues have enormous influence. But peer pressure works both ways. If you have other meditators to talk to, it inspires you to keep going. This doesn't mean you have to join a meditation center, but that positive peer pressure is a powerful prop. Instead of having people take you down, you have peers that lift you up.

I'm a solitary guy, feeling I can do everything on my own. It's a combination of being reserved, and maybe over confident. Finding friends who meditate has been invaluable to me. It has allowed me to share my experiences with others, and to learn from them. This was especially important at first, when I felt alone and baffled about meditation. Talking to others made me realize my questions and problems were not unique. Other people were going through the same things. My friends shared meditation books with me, told me about upcoming teachings, and provided a mirror for me to assess my practice.

Meditating with other people is also very helpful. This is when mutual support becomes almost physical. You're sitting together, feeling the presence of those around you. But in this case the support is reciprocal—their presence supports you, your presence supports them. There's a sense of camaraderie, solidarity, even family. Like joining a bridge club, tennis league, or book group, it helps to do things together.

Studies on the power of habit have shown that to change, belief is critical.[19] You have to really believe in something to get in the habit of doing it. In terms of meditation, you have to believe that the habit of mindlessness doesn't serve you, and trust in the benefits of being mindful. Studies also show that the odds of changing improve dramatically if you do your new thing with a group.

All these props add up. They're like the flying buttresses that support the grand cathedrals of Europe. I use props without hesitation because I need all the help I can get. Distraction is a formidable opponent to meditation. In many spiritual traditions, our modern time is referred to as the Dark Age, what the Hindus call *Kali Yuga,* the age of the demon, and Japanese Buddhists call *Mappo,* the degenerate age. People think that this relates to the massive global problems facing this perilous earth. While that's partly true, the Dark Age mainly refers to the most dangerous and insidious demon of them all: distraction. As we saw in the introduction, the big problems "out there" stem from small but constant problems "in here." Our near lust for entertainment, insane busyness, the pursuit of pleasure, and the raging epidemic of distraction are the true demons of this Dark Age. Tangible and intangible props defend us against these little devils.

---

19 See *The Power of Habit: Why We Do What We Do in Life and Business,* by Charles Duhigg, Random House, New York, NY, 2012.

CHAPTER 6

How to Meditate—Phase One

Body

The basic meditation instruction is very simple. It's so simple that people often think, "That's it!? There has to be more to it than this!" Remember, it's the simplicity that ushers in the profundity. Don't forget this. Because we have quick and complex minds, "simple" is often viewed as unsophisticated or even naïve. Calling someone "simple" is not a compliment. We praise speed and complexity, and meditation is slow and simple. In my thesaurus, synonyms for "slow" include "dull, dimwitted, unintelligent, thick, dense, and brainless."

But in the end, complexity doesn't stand a chance against simplicity. Simple disarms complex. It neutralizes it. Simplicity can bring the modern mind to its knees, and you eventually to the meditation cushion, because the sophisticated mind just doesn't know what to do with it. Simplicity forces the complex mind to give up. Because it's so "thick," something simple will drop through superficiality and speed. It cuts through the shallows and reaches the deep.

What do you do when you have to communicate with a simpleton, or a child? You can't use your usual strategies. You have to drop your game and relate to that person on their terms, otherwise there's no relationship. It's the same with meditation. You have to relate to it on its terms.

The simplicity of meditation will show you what really matters, bring depth to your life, and put you in contact with truth. It's like what happens when someone suddenly speaks the truth. There can be all this clever deception flying around, intricate arguments to and fro, but when truth is admitted everything stops. This is why the honest words of a child can stop an adult dead in their tracks. The emperor of complexity has no clothes, and simplicity exposes that truth.

I'm elaborating on this because it is so tempting to spruce up the meditation technique. Our complex mind wants to make it more complicated. Surrender to the simplicity. Let it take you down—in a good way. Don't try to outsmart it. As we will see, there are ways to make the practice your own, to make it personal, but don't touch the technique itself. There's a traditional saying about meditation: it's so simple we don't believe it; it's so easy we don't trust it. Trust and believe, then the ease and simplicity turns into gold.

Remember that relaxation is the fundamental teaching of meditation. When you do something really simple, it automatically helps you relax.

The body phase

Once you get the basics of meditation you'll see how simple it is. In order to be thorough I will describe the technique in detail. This isn't meant to make it complex, but to make it complete. While there are infinite nuances and refinements to the technique, they all boil down to this: sit, breathe, and pay attention. Everything that follows in the next three chapters are footnotes to this basic instruction. By explaining this further, we can better appreciate the depth of this technique.

After a few weeks of meditating, the technique becomes second nature. It's like learning how to walk. At first it's not so simple. One foot has to go in front of the other, and the feet have to move in harmony. If you bang your knees together it doesn't work well. It helps not to walk on your heels or toes, but to set the heel down first, and then roll the foot to lift your body off of your toes. Your hands have to sway in a synchronized fashion. It helps to keep your eyes open, and don't look down. Don't focus on your feet, look ahead. You have to find your balance and you may fall. A few bumps and bruises are normal. You might get discouraged ... Sounds complex. But of course it isn't. Before you know it you're off and running.

It's exactly the same with meditation. With a little practice, the technique becomes automatic. To make the instruction easier I break it down into three phases: the body phase (sit), the breath phase (breathe), and the mind phase (pay attention). These three phases are not mutually exclusive. They interpenetrate and therefore support each other. It's like having a tripod. It's easy to knock something over if it stands on one leg, or even two. But a tripod is really stable.

The body phase is all about posture. Posture is a big deal in meditation. It's said that if you merely take the proper posture, sooner or later you will find yourself meditating. Sogyal Rinpoche says:

> In the West, people tend to be absorbed by what I call "the technology of meditation." The modern world, after all, is fascinated by mechanisms and machines and addicted to purely practical formulas. But by far the most important feature of meditation is not the technique but the spirit: the skillful, inspired and creative way in

which we practice, which could also be called "the posture." ... Talk about posture is not esoteric pedantry; the whole point of assuming a correct posture is to create a more inspiring environment for meditation... Mind and body are interrelated, and meditation arises naturally once your posture and attitude are inspired.[20]

The "technology of meditation" is important to remember when all the details of the technique are presented below. You might be sitting perfectly, breathing correctly, and doing the technique 100 percent. But if you're not actually working with your mind you're not really meditating. If you think that meditation just means applying a technique, the practice will never come to life and transform you. If you've been meditating for a long time and nothing seems to be happening, this could be a part of your problem.

Good posture is like building a solid house. You start from the ground and work your way up. If the foundation is sturdy the walls will be straight and the roof will stay on. Because it's so foundational, and because many nuances of posture relate to all three phases, most of the commentary will be for this first phase. The breath and mind phases are easily described.

When it comes to simplicity, what could be simpler than sitting? But sitting, like simplicity, has power. When people go on strike they often just sit in front of their place of work. "Sit ins" are very effective. "I'm not going to move" exhibits determination and strength. That's what we're going to do in sitting meditation (which is a synonym for formal mindfulness practice). We're going to go on strike against complexity and speed.

Mindfulness interrupts the conditioned responses we have towards our mind and our world. It breaks this bad habit of mindlessness. The posture of sitting represents this "strike." Instead of always giving in to the impulses of our mind to move, we

---

20 See *Glimpse After Glimpse, Daily Reflections on Living and Dying,* by Sogyal Rinpoche, HarperOne, New York, NY, 1995, December 23 entry.

go against this flow with our very posture. Each time we stand up against a habit, or in this case sit down against it, we frustrate a flow of routinized (mindless) behavior. We're blocking the current, the undertow of mindlessness, that's always sucking us into our discursive mind, and away from reality.

This is my daily practice. Every time I feel that urge to check my iPhone, the latest ping on my computer, or to turn on the TV, I stand up to that impulse and resist the temptation. I go on strike, even though it's just a flash. These moments of resistance are like a mini-revolution against the governing forces of distraction. They may seem inconsequential, but these momentary "sit ins" add up. My resistance culminates in an immovability that keeps me centered.

Neuroscience supports this resistance. Every time I'm mindful, I'm laying down new tracks in my brain and shaping synaptic connections. I'm weakening the vice grip of my conditioning. My refusal to give in to mindlessness burns new circuits in my brain that makes it easier for me to be mindful in the future. This is why mindfulness gets easier the more I practice it. And this is why it's so hard initially. With my mindfulness practice I'm re-wiring my brain. I'm changing my default setting from mindlessness to mindfulness, and my very posture facilitates that.

For the complex mind, being taught how to sit properly is patronizing. It's an offense to our sophistication. This is when you need to let go of your concepts. Trust the method that has been handed down for thousands of years and successfully practiced by countless people. Then ask yourself: has my conventional approach to life worked? Have I been able to think my way into happiness? Does my speed and complexity make me happy? Give it up. Or at least question it. Try a new approach.

Sitting is the adult version of "time out." When your child misbehaves, you might call a "time out." The child has to sit still until they settle. Little Billy will fidget like crazy, but he's not allowed to get up. When we sit in meditation we're calling "time out" on the mischievous mind. Until big Bill learns how to settle, he will fidget with equal discomfort.

Mental posture

Before I turn to the details of physical posture, let's discuss the importance of mental "posture," or attitude. The interplay between the physical and the mental is a central ingredient in meditation. On one level, body and mind are obviously different. But on a deeper level, as meditation will show you, they are not. The point is that what you do with your body has a profound effect on your mind, and what you do with your mind has a profound effect on your body. This is one reason why yoga is such a terrific preparation for meditation.

In terms of mental posture, the foundational attitude is that when you sit down to meditate you're taking your seat in the world. It's a noble and dignified attitude, almost regal. There's a sense of strength and stability. You are taking your throne and about to rule the kingdom of your own mind. It's not an arrogant posture, but a confident one. Nothing is going to move you. This attitude of immovability will help you stabilize your body, which then helps you stabilize your mind. So even though the mind phase is formally the third phase of the technique, it's informally the ground for all three. You use your mind to help your body to help your mind. Body and mind prop each other up.

Earlier we saw that meditation is about stopping and seeing. The stopping part begins quite literally with sitting. To stop the mind from running around (phase three), you stop the body from running around (phase one), and you stop your speech (phase two). With these two brakes, the mind will naturally slow down.

What we're doing with mental and physical posture is creating the proper environment. If the environment is there, meditation just happens. Meditation can be viewed as a kind of climate control, setting the proper climate with our body, speech, and mind. It's like trying to go to sleep. If you want to go to sleep you might drink warm milk, set the temperature just right, and shut down external distractions. You then assume the proper posture, cover yourself up, and eventually fall asleep. If you set it up, sleep just happens. It's the same with meditation. The only difference is that in this case you're trying to "wake up." Phase one and phase two of the technique are the set up for waking up.

To demonstrate the power of posture, try this experiment. Close your eyes. Notice whatever you're thinking or feeling. Don't change anything. With a subtle change in posture you are about to change your mind. Raise the corners of your lips. Smile. What happens to your mind? Doesn't your mind also smile? The posture of meditation is designed to make your mind smile. It takes more effort than just grinning, but it also produces a bigger and more durable "smile."

Dr. Paul Ekman is an expert on facial expression. When he was doing his research he would assume facial expressions for days on end. He discovered that these minor alterations in facial posture had major alterations in his mood. For example, when he replicated the expressions associated with sadness, he found himself getting sad. Body and mind are not the same, nor are they different.

Meditation is a downer

The emphasis on the body is largely about coming down to earth. Our body is our personal earth. Body is what grounds us, and maintains our contact with the stability and sanity of the literal earth. It keeps us real.

So much of our stress comes from always being up. We're always under pressure to catch up, keep up, or hurry up. We're constantly speeding up, cranking it up, and therefore heating up. We're uptight, upset, shook up and all wound up from all the up-heavals of life. We're so up that we have a hard time falling down into sleep, let alone into meditation.

The necktie is a wonderful symbol for choking ourselves off from our body (the earth), our emotions, and our hearts. As Western business ideals spread across the world, and busyness comes with it, it's fascinating to watch the necktie spread as well. Men all over the world have given up their indigenous attire to lift themselves into the modern world with the necktie. But so often the necktie turns into a noose.

When men come home from work they undo their neckties and begin to relax. They start to come down. Maybe it takes a drink, or the TV. When we meditate we go even further by un-doing our mental "neckties," and start to drop into the wisdom of our body. Meditation cools us down, calms us down, and settles us down by allowing us to descend from our head into our body. We quiet down and then we keep it down by slowing down.

From a different angle, we all like to get high. Whether it's al-cohol, drugs, sports, or the buzz of entertainment, we're addicted to our uppers. There's an urge to escape that often underlies this need to be high. Up often implies out. It's a way to disconnect from the harsh reality of earthly matters, or anything that gets us down. There's nothing inherently wrong in wanting to be up for things, for cheering up or living it up. You want to be up, but in the correct manner. As we will see when we return to the instruc-tions on physical posture, you literally want to be upright, or up in the right way.

Nothing can stay up forever, that's the problem. And if we're too up, or manic, we're eventually going to crash down. We eventually get sick. Stressed out people are forced down into their bodies when they get ill, for that's where healing occurs. As the mind drops back into the body it reunites with it, and this non-duality cures. It's like putting a cast on a broken bone. The fractured parts naturally heal when they're held together.

The word "meditation" can be traced to a number of roots (to ponder; measure; reflect upon; think about), and according to some sources shares the same root with the word "medicine," which is the Latin verb medeor, meaning "heal, cure, or remedy." Meditation as medication therefore has an etymological basis. Both are designed to heal.

Just like there's a place for being up, there's also a place for being down. In Shambhala Buddhism they talk about "the genuine heart of sadness." This is sadness in its truest sense, where sad originally meant "having enough, being sated." When you drop into the wisdom of your body, through meditation or yoga, you will find everything you need and want. You will discover a level of inner satisfaction that has eluded you.

Many people talk about meditation and its role on the spiritual path in terms of "waking up." It's a synonym for enlightenment. But meditation is more about "waking down." You're not trying to get up and out, you're trying to drop down and in. Emphasizing the body points us in this right direction. We also talk about "growing up," which takes on literal meaning as we physically grow in childhood. But the meditative and spiritual paths are more about "growing down," or "growing in," which takes on literal meaning as we enter old age. This is the growth that takes place if someone ages gracefully, and is willing to learn the difficult lessons of letting go. Growing down is the growth of maturity.

A consequence of all this descent is not depression, but simplicity. Everything becomes extra-ordinary. It's so refreshing and liberating. In my experience, the most accomplished meditators are the most humble and ordinary. They have gotten down to it, and are so happy staying down—because that's where they find real happiness.

Physical posture

Let's return to the physical posture. I'll describe it first from the point of view of sitting on a meditation cushion, and then adjust the instructions for sitting on a chair. Even though there are a number of aspects to this posture, the basic idea is to assume an attentive posture. It's like the posture you would naturally take while listening to a good lecture. Your body is upright and attentive, which naturally invites an upright and attentive mind.

Contemplation - Body-mind

Close your eyes. As with the smile meditation, just notice your mind. Now bring your body into an attentive posture. Pull your shoulders back, lift your head, and straighten your spine. Hold this upright posture for a few minutes and observe your mind. Now slump. Drop your head and shoulders, and slouch over. Hold this saggy posture for a few minutes and observe your mind. What do you notice? Go back and forth between these postures. What does the posture of your body do to the posture of your mind?

The breakdown of the technique into body, breath, and mind allows us to work our way up from the ground of meditation (body) to its fruit (mind). When you take your seat in meditation, you can imagine yourself planted like a majestic redwood. With roots deep into the ground, and a straight and stable trunk, you can weather anything that blows across the upper branches (see figures 2 and 3, pages 98 and 99).

Begin by sitting on the middle of your meditation cushion. Center yourself on the cushion. Don't sit too far forward or too far back. Feel your connection to the stability of the earth. Cross your legs, which are like a miniature root system connecting you firmly to the ground. Rest your hands on top of your thighs, not too far over the knee, which would pull you forward, nor too close to your body, which would push you back. This is the bottom third of the posture, which is all about grounding yourself.

Next we move up to the trunk. In order for the posture to grow properly, it must be kept upright. Keep your spine firm but not stiff. A sturdy trunk represents the masculine quality of fearlessness, the sense of immovability. Nothing can blow you over. But this strong back is balanced with a soft front. Keep your chest and heart open and receptive, which represents the feminine quality of gentleness. This is done by pulling your shoulders back, exposing your heart. If you just expose your heart, most of the posture comes together under this central gesture. It's literally and figuratively the heart of the posture.

Fearlessness and gentleness are two central ingredients in meditation. You have to be brave, but kind, to meditate. This is the middle third of the posture, which is about strength and kindness.

Finally we move up to the branches. I like the term "branches" for this top third of the body phase because it lessens the importance we usually give to our heads. While we obviously have to use all three aspects of the body phase, the most important aspects are the roots and the trunk. You can pull off a flower, and even trim a stem, but if the roots are intact the rest of the plant will always return. Set the foundation properly and the rest will naturally follow.

Figure 2

As for this branch phase of the posture, keep your head aligned directly above your spinal column. This often means tucking your head in slightly. Many people move through the world headfirst and headstrong—"heading" in the wrong direction. When my meditation instructor pointed out how far forward my head was when I sat, I was shocked. It was a humbling symbol of how I lead my life with my concepts.

In meditation there's a sense of "good head and shoulders." It's almost military in its up-rightness. This often means pulling our shoulders back. Because of the weight of the world, many of us hunch over. Stooping could also be a defensive posture to protect our hearts. We've been hurt. Hearts have been broken. So we shield ourselves.

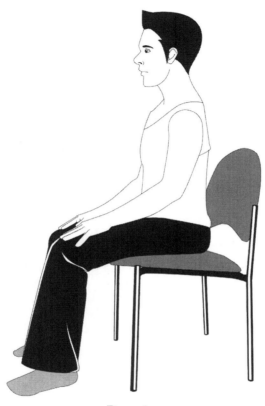

Figure 3

In meditation we want to lighten up and open up, two of the best ways to be up. By lifting and opening physically, we invite ourselves to do so psychologically. By pulling our head back and lifting our shoulders, we're shedding loads of psychological baggage. It's almost like someone has jumped on our back and we're gently but firmly saying, "get off!" If you hunch over, things will land on your upper back and shoulders. If you sit up straight, they will slide off like snow on a steep roof.

Being "straight up" is also the posture of honesty, another ingredient in meditation. You can't be crooked and practice meditation. In ancient India, the wise Rishis were literally "the straight ones," those who always spoke the truth. Meditation invites you to be straight with yourself, and by sitting straight up you're embodying this quality. Self-deception doesn't have a place to land if you're straight with yourself.

In this practice your eyes are open. You're looking slightly down at an angle of about 45 degrees. The visual field is soft, receptive, and unfocused. An open gaze invites an open mind. The deep connection between our physical eye and our mind's eye becomes visible in meditation.

People often associate meditation with closed eyes. There are pros and cons to having your eyes open or shut. Having your eyes open may be more difficult at first, and therefore slightly more advanced. But it represents that you're not trying to hide from anything. You're not closing your eyes and running from the world, or from yourself. Leave all your senses open. Look directly at whatever arises, while not allowing yourself to get involved with it. Meditation is about accommodation, and having your eyes open represents that. You're not creating an antiseptic situation, with no germs of distraction or obstacles. You're staying open to whatever arises, and learning how to relate to it properly.

If you're sensitive to outside distractions, it's okay to close your eyes for a while to gather yourself. Once you're settled, gently open your eyes. If you find your mind is wild, lower your gaze. If your mind is heavy or dull, raise your gaze. It's like fine-tuning a violin, finding that middle way "tone" between too tight and too loose. After you've been meditating for some time, experiment with your gaze, without entertaining yourself, to see how your physical eye affects your mind's eye.

Getting drowsy in meditation is a common problem. It's harder to fall asleep if your eyes are open. Having your eyes open also helps with post-meditation. A big part of meditation is bringing the meditative mind to daily life, mixing meditation and post-meditation. Most of us don't go through life with our eyes closed. So even though meditating with eyes open may be a bit harder at first, it's better in the long run. We're trying to "wake up" and come into the world properly. We're not trying to enter some trancelike state.

Conversely, meditating with closed eyes may be easier at first. There's nothing wrong with meditating with your eyes closed, the emphasis is just different. Closed eyes help to settle the mind, and conveys a sense of letting go of external distractions. But because we associate closed eyes with sleep, it does affect our alertness. When you leave your meditation, it's also harder to transition the meditative mind into daily life. If you associate meditation with closed eyes, and life with open eyes, it's more difficult to mix the two. For all these reasons I recommend that you meditate with your eyes open.

The last step in the posture is to place your tongue against the backside of your upper front teeth, and to keep your lips slightly parted, as if you were whispering the word "ah." These subtle points bring a sense of mindful refinement to the posture. Placing your tongue up there also inhibits salivary flow, so you don't have to swallow all the time. Even though it's better to breathe through your nose, parting your lips helps you breathe through your mouth if you need to. It's also more relaxed than a "tight lipped" approach.

There are infinite refinements, but these are the basics. When you first start to sit, sooner or later you'll experience some aches and pains. Our bodies are often as inflexible as our minds. So while this posture is very gentle, it can bring out our mental and physical rigidity. You'll get an itch here, an ache there or a cramp.

You want to relate to these potential distractions with a "middle way" approach. Unless it's an intense cramp, or something that requires immediate movement, feel into the sensation and explore it for a moment. Don't just reflexively move to make yourself immediately comfortable. Establish a *relationship* to the sensation.

After a few moments do what you need to do to lessen the discomfort. Don't entertain yourself with it. The point isn't to tough it out or even hurt yourself. The point is to be kind to yourself, but not to immediately indulge every impulse. If your knees or ankles get sore, uncross your legs and lift them up. Rest your hands on top of your knees. After practicing for a few weeks or months your body will get more flexible (along with your mind). It gets physically easier to sit. Muscles stretch out, circulation changes, and your body adapts. Once again, most of the effort, and discomfort, comes at the beginning.

When I did my first month long group retreat, I didn't follow any of this advice. There were fifty of us, and we all had assigned seats. Mine was in the front row. Because I knew lots of people could see me, I developed a ridiculous approach to my posture. I vowed I would never move, which would convey my "advanced" status to the group. I would get an itch, but wouldn't move to scratch. My knees or ankles would start to ache, but I didn't move. This approach was actually a demonstration of my stupidity and inexperience. They only thing it conveyed was my pathetic pride.

Because there are so many diseases and individual quirks, it's impossible to cover all the possible variations. The bottom line is that the posture is completely workable. As long as you have a mind you can meditate. A proper posture just helps. Don't use your physical limitations as an excuse. Yes, it may be more difficult if you have artificial joints or a bad back, but there are ways to work with any situation.

If you're sitting in a chair it's easy to adapt these instructions. In this case you don't cross your legs. You plant your feet squarely on the ground. Pull away from the back of the chair, so you're not leaning against it. This is another metaphor: you're not leaning against anything or anyone. You're cultivating and relying on your own inner strength and support. Every other aspect of the instruction remains the same.

Feel to change

Do you remember our poor frog from Chapter One, the one who got boiled alive? The problem with the frog, and with most of us, is the loss of *feeling*. For most of us, thinking has conquered feeling. The head, which rests in physical preeminence on top of our body, has dominated the body. It literally and figuratively looks down on the feeling body. Even though thinking about something can lead to change, if you really want to change, something has to touch you. You have to feel it.

Feeling takes place in your body, in your guts or your heart. Not in your head. The brain, where scientists say thinking takes place, ironically doesn't have pain receptors and literally can't feel anything. This is why neurosurgeons can do open brain surgery on a fully conscious patient and not hurt them. The brain is literally out of touch.

By relying so much on our thinking brain we have put ourselves out of touch—with ourselves, with others, and with reality. This is important, because we can't think our way out of every problem. Science, logic, and rationality can't solve everything. The eminent physicist David Bohm said, "It looks as if the thing we use to solve our problems with [thinking] is the source of our problems." We can't think our way out of every problem when uncontrolled thinking is itself the problem. Runaway thinking has gotten us into this mess. It will not get us out.

To get out of this mess, the speed and stress of modern life, we have to get back to our bodies. To leap out of these hot waters we first have to feel them. This is why getting back in touch with our bodies is so important, and another reason I emphasize the body in meditation.

In meditation we finally come to our senses. Literally and figuratively. That's where the present moment is fully felt. That's where we get back in touch. You can't feel the past or future, you can only feel now. You can't see, smell, taste or hear the past or future. You can only sense the present moment. So by using the natural wisdom of our senses—our body—we're getting back in touch. If there's a mantra for this book, it is this: more in the body, less in the head.

Please understand, I'm not against thinking. I love to think. The issue is a proper relationship to thought. Without the ability to think we couldn't skillfully implement our feelings. We obviously need thought to function. It's a question of balance. For most of us, we put too much weight into our thinking. Our heads are so full of thoughts that they ache, or tip us forward. I'm always correcting my posture as I sit, stand, or walk, by tucking my head back in and exposing more of my heart. That I literally go through life headfirst is a symbol of the excessive importance I give to my thoughts.

If you think too much, you will lose contact. If you feel too much, you will get lost in mushy emotionality and never get anything done. Thinking and feeling need to complement each other, not insult each other. Thinking without feeling is blind. Feeling without thinking is lame. To see and move properly we need both working in harmony. For most of us, creating this harmony means less head and more heart/body.

CHAPTER 7

How to Meditate—Phase Two

Breath

Once you've set the ground with your body, you begin to focus on your breath. The instruction here is very simple: bring your awareness to the natural movement of your breath. Rather than "watching" it, feel the breath going out, feel it coming in. You don't visualize it, you don't think about it, you feel it. It's as if your awareness is riding on the movement of your breath.

You're not concentrating one hundred percent on your breath. That's too tight. But you're also not sloppily following your breath now and again. That's too loose. You're gently but precisely aware of your breathing. Give it about 25% of your attention, and let the other 75% relax. That's the instruction for the breath phase.

To give it some weight, let's explore this second phase and bring new meaning to breath. Again, this isn't meant to make it more complex, but to help you appreciate the depth of the technique. If something is too simple our complex minds may dismiss it.

First of all, most people tend to think about their breath instead of feel it. Studies have actually shown this, and it's another example of how we're losing our ability to feel things, even something as ordinary as our breath.[21] Because the sensation is so subtle, the instruction to follow our breath is an invitation to touch into our bodies at a more subtle level, "forcing" us to stay in contact with our body as we move from the body phase to the mind phase. We're asked to pay attention to how our breath feels, in our nose, our diaphragm, even our lungs. It's almost like the instruction is telling us, "stay in touch (with your body), don't go away" as you transition into the more ephemeral mind phase, which tends to be the most disembodied phase. As your practice matures, allow yourself to slowly identify with your breath, as if you were becoming one with it. Eventually the breath, the breather, and the breathing unite in a form of non-duality.

While the body phase is mostly about stability and stillness, the breath introduces movement. This is important because even though meditation cultivates stillness, stillness itself isn't the point. It's just part of it. The point is to find stillness in anything, even movement. If stillness was the only point, we would end up wrestling with our moving mind, trying to pin it down to the present moment. Thoughts become the enemy. We would also lose our meditation the minute we got off the cushion, so there would be no chance of mixing meditation and life.

Equating meditation exclusively with stillness also tends to put meditation in opposition to daily life, which is chock full of activity. You have the stillness of your meditation and the busyness of your life, never the twain shall meet. This is a constricted definition of meditation that guarantees frustration.

We start meditation with an emphasis on stillness, as represented in the stillness of our body, but progress is marked by mixing stillness and motion. The fruit of meditation is preferring

21 Judson Brewer, MD, PhD., Assistant Professor of Psychiatry and Medical Director, Yale Therapeutic Neuroscience Clinic at the Yale School of Medicine.

neither. It doesn't matter if you're sitting or moving. You can meditate with anything. Once you understand the principles of meditation, as nurtured in stillness, it's easy to extend those principles into movement.

By working with our breath in meditation we're starting to develop a healthy relationship to movement at its most elementary level. There's no problem with movement in meditation. The problem is getting swept up in it. As we will see below, this is important because when we get to the mind phase we're working with the movement of thoughts, which is an even more subtle form of relating properly to movement. That's when getting carried away with movement is a big deal. So with the breath phase we're preparing for this more subtle relationship to movement.

Because it's so constant and automatic, we take our breath for granted. But hold your breath under water for a minute and you'll see how precious it is. It's more valuable than gold. When you get down to it, you would give everything you own for another breath. If a billionaire was about to suffocate, he wouldn't hesitate to give his fortune for a few more breaths. Relating to our breath in meditation helps us appreciate its value. It helps us appreciate life.

Breath is life itself. If someone is alive it means they're breathing. We are literally one breath away from death. Breathe out, don't breathe in, and you're dead. Breathing is also a teaching for how we should relate to everything we think we own, for every breath we take has to be given back. You can't live on inhalation alone, as inspiring as it is.

Your breath can show you that you don't really own anything. Everything you feel you own, even your body, is just a fleeting loan. When you die it's all given back. Even the elements of your body are returned to the lender, mother earth. In Sanskrit, it's considered impolite to say someone has died. It's more considerate to say "pancatvam gatah:" "they have returned to fiveness"—to the five elements of earth, water, fire, wind, and space. You may grasp after things and thoughts the way you gasp after air, but neither is yours to own.

Even though we get energy from food, most of our energy comes from breathing. You can go for weeks without eating, and days without drinking. But you can barely go a few minutes without breathing. Sprint for ten seconds and you'll quickly realize how breath is the energy of life.

Breath is also a bridge between body and mind, which is why it fits so nicely between the body phase and the mind phase. Breath shares qualities of both. It's obviously connected to the body. We can physically feel our breath. It has a kind of form. But breath is also formless, which is more like the mind. While breath can touch you, you can't really touch it. This is another instance of why working with our breath is a pathway into working with our mind. It connects form and formlessness.

There is an intimate connection between the movement of breath and the movement of mind. When you're angry, notice how shallow, rapid, and choppy your breath is. When you lust after something, notice how you pant. I have heard that depressed people exhibit superficial breathing. It's almost like they're partly dead because they're not fully infusing their bodies with the breath of life. When you're really calm, notice how your breath is even and settled. This information can help you whenever you're scared, nervous, or angry. Just take a few deep breaths.

In my part-time practice of dentistry, I often use breath as a potent form of sedation, even anesthesia. I can tell if someone is anxious about getting an injection by observing their rapid and shallow breathing. Sometimes they're on the verge of hyperventilating, or passing out. To calm them down I instruct them to take slow deep breaths with me. I place my reassuring hand on their shoulder as we breathe together, and then slowly deepen their breathing as they synchronize with my own. The effect is remarkable, and as effective as many sedatives. In less than a minute they've dropped out of their panic-stricken mind and into their body.

Some meditators can calm their minds down to the point that they literally stop breathing. Again, stopping thoughts is not the point of meditation. But if you do stop the movement of your thoughts you will stop the movement of your breath. When you witness something extraordinarily beautiful or shocking, it can also stop your mind and literally take your breath away. I remember listening to the legendary pianist Vladimir Horowitz as he tore into a stunning encore. It was literally breathtaking.

Breath and Space

The modern mind has no space in it. Thoughts are packed into our heads like junk in a trash compactor. Meditation ventilates the mind. We mix our mind with space, and breathing represents that mixing. Remember the feeling of being stressed out about something, then finally resolving it? You breathe a big sigh of relief. It's like that. Meditation allows the mind to take a deep breath and relax.

Working with our breath is like installing mental air-conditioning. Feeling the cool breath chills out our overheated minds. The influx of space, represented by our breath, has this cooling effect. Imagine being in a crowded subway on a sweltering summer day. The claustrophobia is inflammatory. Now imagine stepping into a spacious air-conditioned room. You immediately open and relax. It's that kind of feeling. This is part of the internal climate control of meditation.

"Spirit" comes from a root word that means "breath." Spirituality is the art and science of proper breathing. From pranayama practice in Hinduism, to lungta (wind horse) practices in Buddhism, to modern Holotropic breath work—wherever you find spirit you will find breath.

In some esoteric traditions breath is referred to as "wind," and considered the most powerful of all forces. Not only does it inspire and expire individual life, it also creates and destroys entire world systems. When we unwind with meditation it's as if we're un-winding. And as we learn how to feel the inflation of our lungs by becoming mindful of our breathing, we discover that we're deflating all the windy thoughts in our heads. It is also taught that as one gains complete control over the inner wind (*prana*—which is very subtle "breath"), one gains control over the outer wind.

Contemplation - Breath-mind

Take a breath and hold it for as long as you comfortably can. Now extend that hold beyond your comfort range. Ordinary breathing becomes extraordinarily important. Do the same thing with an outbreath. Does your expensive car or house come close to the value of a single breath? To see how the movement of breath relates to the movement of mind, hold your breath again and this time watch your mind. Do you have more or less thoughts when you're holding your breath? Now take short rapid breaths, but be careful not to hyperventilate. What do you notice now? Take five slow and deep breaths. What does this do to your mind? Finally, extend the gap between the in-breath and the out-breath—what do you notice?

Just like with the body, breath is not the same as the mind, but it's also not totally different. By working with your breath in phase two you're also working with your mind. Once again, it's the tripod effect, with each phase interpenetrating and supporting the other.

The more I meditate the more I realize the connection between inner and outer. I live on the front range of Colorado where the weather changes frequently and dramatically. One minute it's sunny and warm, within an hour it's stormy and cold. Rain, sleet, fog, hail, snow and sun can all happen in the same day. When I woke up in a funk the other day, it also happened to be foggy. When the fog lifted I noticed that my dark mood lifted. Outer and inner weather has connections deeper than mere analogy.

By working with our breath we're starting to establish a relationship to the inner space of our mind, and to "wind." By discovering this inner silence and space, then learning to rest in it, we realize that all our thoughts and emotions, just like the weather, come and go within this space. Lightening and anger can flash in space, rain and the tears of sorrow are held within space, sunshine and happiness are easily accommodated in this space. The only thing that's constant, that holds everything yet remains untouched by it, is space itself—the silent awareness below all thought.

When you become familiar with this inner space, and eventually identify with it (and not all the thoughts and emotions that come and go within it), you become indestructible like space. Then it doesn't matter what blows in and out of your mind. Just as space is unaffected by weather, your mind is unaffected by thoughts and emotions.

Finally, while the vast majority of people do fine with coming back to their breath in meditation, there could be some who just can't relate to their breathing. Perhaps they have respiratory problems, or other difficult relationships to breath. In those rare instances you can replace the anchor of breathing with an external object, or with feeling into your body. If you choose to focus on an object, like a candle, then that is what you come back to when your mind strays. If you choose to come back to your body as the focal object of meditation, then you could make your focus the sensation of your hands resting on your thighs, or your buttocks on the cushion. It's easy to replace your breath with some other focal point. While breath is the classic object of meditation, we need to remember that mindfulness is the point—not the object used to get you there. Trungpa Rinpoche said, "It's not a question of forcing the mind back to some particular object, but of bringing it back down from the dream world into reality."

When you're meditating, don't think about all these details and subtleties. Just breathe. Paralysis by analysis, overthinking the technique, is a potential trap. If some of these connections come to mind, that's fine. But don't get carried away with them. These details should augment your meditation, not distract you from it.

CHAPTER 8

How to Meditate—Phase Three

Mind

With phase one and two of the instruction we're sitting and breathing. That's it. What could be simpler? We have created the proper root and stem from which the flower of meditation can now blossom. As with the other two phases, I will give the technique for phase three first then provide some commentary.

The basic instruction for phase three is simple. Whenever anything distracts you from your breath, mentally say to yourself "thinking," and return to the breath. Whether it's a thought, an image, an anticipation, regret, or feeling doesn't matter. Whatever steals your awareness away from your breath is labeled "thinking." If it's something external, like a distracting sound or smell, the same instruction applies. Notice the sound or smell, but don't let it distract you. Saying "thinking" is not an act of squashing the distraction. It's an act of recognizing it. "Thinking" is gentle yet precise, like popping a mental energy bubble (thought) with a feather. Something distracts you ... "thinking" ... return to the breath. Something else distracts you ... "thinking" ... return to the breath. That's the instruction for phase three.

There's so much that can be said about this phase. This is where the action is. First of all, "thinking" is not saying "bad." This is a common mistake that quickly leads to the inaccurate assessment: "I'm a bad meditator. I have so many thoughts." Mentally saying "thinking" is actually a good thing. It means you're finally starting to see what's going on in your mind. "Thinking" is a moment of awareness, it's the awareness part of mindfulness-awareness meditation. Every time you say "thinking" you're exercising the awareness muscle, which gets increasingly stronger. This is how meditation develops this most treasured quality. Labeling also helps us see the qualities of our experience, without getting sucked into the content.

"Thinking" is part of the instruction to "touch-and-go." We touch thoughts by recognizing them as thinking and then we let them go. There will be times when we don't want to let them go. Thoughts can be very entertaining, and turning off the "TV" can be difficult. The Cinemax of the mind has endless movies to seduce you into the theater of distraction, even though most of them are re-runs. This is when we need to gently remind ourselves that meditation does require some discipline, and that this is not the time to indulge thoughts. We might even smile at ourselves when we feel the temptation to be carried away, and say "I've seen this movie before."

Through the act of recognition (awareness) you're starting to establish a relationship to your thoughts. Once again, it's hard to have a relationship to something you can't see. So the "seeing" part of "stop and see" is already happening. Every time you notice a distraction you've already come back to awareness. "Thinking" just acknowledges that. Each time you awaken to not being present is paradoxically a moment of presence. If you realize you are not there, that means you are there. So recognizing that you've been distracted is a cause for rejoicing—not reprimand.

As we've seen, there's nothing bad about thoughts, feelings, or anything that arises in meditation. They're never the problem. Improper relationship is the problem. At this level that means being seduced, revolted, or defined by whatever arises. We're either sucked into our thoughts and emotions, turned off by them, or identify with them. When we say "thinking" in meditation we're not slapping our mind. We're simply acknowledging that the mind has strayed into one of these detours or dead ends. Saying "thinking" simultaneously acknowledges that we've been derailed from the present moment, and puts us back on the track of nowness.

Mindfulness-awareness tends to thoughts and emotions with acceptance and equanimity. It shows you how to love your mind. There's no need to change your thoughts, or get rid of them, if you realize they don't define you. For example, let's say you have the thought that you're a loser. If you buy into it and indulge that thought or feeling by digging up all the "proof" of other similar thoughts, you have just ensured your suffering. Meditation shows you that you are not your thoughts or emotions. They do not define you.

Thoughts are only a problem when we make them a problem. Left alone they are harmless movements of the mind, like campfire sparks dissolving into the night sky. It's only when we follow, and therefore feed, our thoughts that they ignite all kinds of issues. That fleeting thought of your boss, if followed and fed, can spark a fantasy about how you want to strangle him. But if it's recognized and released, that thought evaporates on the spot. A feeling of desire, if followed and fed, can trigger an avalanche of emotion. But if it's recognized and released, it melts on contact. Meditation works with radical acceptance. Let thoughts come and let them go—like the imprint of a bird flying through the sky.

If a thought isn't recognized, it will link into another thought, then another, and gets bigger and stronger. Instead of bringing your attention back to your breath, indulging in a thought feeds it. You give it a life it doesn't inherently have. Your indulgence is like wind that blows a tiny ripple into a tidal wave.

Not a fix

We have to be careful how we use the label "thinking" because one of the most sinister obstacles to meditation is unwittingly using it to try to fix ourselves. Meditation is about acceptance, openness, and unconditional love. You're not trying to fix anything. You're loving yourself—just the way you are. It's easy to misunderstand the label "thinking" as a corrective maneuver. There may be a subtle sense of rejection when you notice your thinking and return to your breath. But you're not rejecting your thoughts. You're just recognizing them and coming back to your breath. Meditation is about unfixing, not fixing. Fixation, at any level or definition, is the problem—not the solution.

We could add this to our list of what meditation is not: it's not a quick fix. It's not quick and it's not a fix. It won't fix you because there's nothing wrong with you. And it's not quick. In our culture of instant gratification and speed, meditation is a real drag. It's meant to be. You've thrown the anchor overboard and it will eventually slow you down, calm you down, and keep you down on the present moment.

When I started meditating I was certain that thoughts were the enemy. Meditation was like hunting. A thought would arise and when I saw it I would take aim and shoot. "Thinking" was like pulling the trigger. "Bang!"—another one bites the dust. Because of my aggressive attitude I totally missed the point. I forgot that meditation is the practice of kindness.

Thoughts, like breath, are just natural movements. That's what the mind does. The wind blows, the river flows, and the mind thinks. Don't try to stop the wind, dam the water, or block your thoughts. Let nature flow. You're not building a dam. You're building a boat. You're learning how to float on top of these currents of thought, but without letting them carry you away. That's the practice.

The movement of the mind only becomes a problem when it sucks you in. Subconscious thoughts are like an undertow. If a thought arises and pulls you in, it's back to the same old story. At that point you're not meditating. You're drowning in unrecognized thought. But if that same thought arises and you label it "thinking," it evaporates. Same thought, different relationship.

Let's say you're meditating and the thought of your boss pops up. If you catch it and say "thinking," you're free. But if you don't catch it, that thought will catch you. Before you know it you're caught up in endless story lines about your boss. A few minutes might pass before you realize you've been snagged. At that point don't beat yourself up. Everybody gets lost in thought. Smile at the fact that you've been caught, say "thinking," and return to your breath.

While meditation can temporarily stop the chain of thoughts, and that's good in terms of being able to experience a new quality of mind, that's not the point. If thoughts happen to stop in meditation, that's great. If they don't, that's also great. The biggest benefit of working with your thoughts, or experiencing a cessation of thought, is that it introduces you to a new dimension of the mind. You can actually have an experience without thinking about it. It also puts thoughts in a new perspective. They're finally seen for what they actually are—harmless movements of the mind.

The power of perspective

In Chapter Three we talked about "the witness," and introduced the theme of perspective, a topic we'll return to later when we talk about view. Perspective is everything. Where you "stand" in relation to something, mentally or physically, dictates your experience of it. Philosophically, what position you take on an issue changes everything. Just ask any politician.

If you're too close to something (physically or mentally), you'll never see it properly. If you're too far away, you won't see it at all. Meditation provides proper perspective because it gives you a new place to stand, one that allows you to see your thoughts and emotions in a new and liberating light. The Greek mathematician Archimedes famously said, "Give me a place to stand and I will move the earth." Give me a place to take new mental stand, and the leverage of this stance (perspective) can similarly move the earth, or at least my relationship to it.

Right now we're too close to our thoughts and emotions. They have all the leverage, so they move us. Meditation offers the stance that switches the tables in this power play. With a meditative and therefore liberating standpoint, thoughts no longer have the power to move us, unless we allow the movement. We can be moved to act upon a thought or emotion if we wish, like allowing compassion to move us, but because meditation reverses the leverage, the contents of our mind no longer have the power to move us without our permission.

Here's another analogy. I love to fly on overcast days because it reminds me of the power of perspective. When I'm on the ground looking up, things don't look so good. It's dark and gloomy and the forecast is grim. But when the plane cuts through the clouds and ascends above them, my new perspective changes everything. My transcendent view allows me to perceive, and therefore relate, to the same clouds in a dramatically different way. From below they were dark and forbidding; from above they are luminous and even welcoming.

Earlier we talked about meditation in terms of "stop and see." Stopping is not necessarily stopping thoughts, but stopping your inappropriate relationship to them, and therefore removing their leverage over you. Stop your usual relationship and you'll be able to see. A usual relationship pulls you away from what's really happening, and mucks everything up. A meditative relationship brings you back to what's really happening, and clears everything up.

When you first start meditating it's common to say "thinking" all the time. It's almost like a mantra: "thinking, thinking, thinking." You never knew you had so many thoughts. People sometimes say that meditation increases thoughts. It doesn't. You're simply observing them clearly for the first time. "Seeing" is already happening. The Sri Lankan monk Bhante Gunaratana wrote:

> Somewhere in this process, you will come face to face with the sudden and shocking realization that you are completely crazy. Your mind is a shrieking, gibbering madhouse on wheels barreling pell-mell down the hill, utterly out of control and helpless. No problem. You are not crazier than you were yesterday. It has always been this way, and you just never noticed. You are also no crazier than everybody else around you. The only real difference is that you have confronted the situation; they have not. So they still feel relatively comfortable. That does not mean that they are better off. Ignorance may be bliss, but it does not lead to liberation. So don't let this realization unsettle you. It is a milestone actually, a sign of real progress. The very fact that you have looked at the problem straight in the eye means that you are on your way up and out of it.[22]

---

22 See *Mindfulness in Plain English*, by Bhante Henepola Gunaratana, Wisdom Publications, Boston, MA, 2011.

Beginners often complain, "I'm not meditating, I'm just saying 'thinking' all the time." But that *is* the meditation. If you're frustrated, that means your definition of meditation is too limited. You still think meditation means getting rid of thoughts. Because *seeing* is the second phase of meditation, we might think that we have to fully *stop* before we can see. But the first level of stopping and seeing happens the minute we sit down. Seeing that you have all these thoughts is a really good thing. With this perspective you can start to relate to them properly.

The canvas

The meditation technique is like a blank canvas. It provides a background upon which you can now "paint" your mind. In other words, being instructed to sit and breath is the white canvas. When you sit and breathe (the stopping part), your thoughts suddenly stand out (the seeing part). It's like what happens when you lie down to sleep. Thoughts suddenly pop out more clearly and seem to multiply. Movement always stands out in contrast to stillness. Noise always appears in contrast to silence. In other words, perception is always generated in contrast.

You see these black letters because they stand out against the white background of the page. In the technique of meditation, sitting and breathing provides the white page. If the page was grey, which is akin to the busyness of life, you wouldn't see very much of your mind. Because you're moving as much as your thoughts, there's no contrast. You're blind to most of what's going on in your mind. One scientist says that we're unaware of 99% of what occurs in our mind.[23] Stop, however, and you will see.

But *contrast does not mean opposition*. The fact that thoughts stand out *against* the background of silence and stillness doesn't

---

23 Bruce Lipton, PhD; see www.lifetrainings.com/Your-unconscious-mind-is-running-you-life.html. Accessed January 3, 2014.

mean that thoughts are opposed to stillness. Thoughts are not against stillness in that regard. They are in opposition to stillness only in terms of perception. In other words, in our ability to see them.

This may seem like a technical detail or word play, but it's a practical and important point. It's a reason people quit meditating. It's a reason why meditators feel that thoughts are bad, and that good meditation means thought-free meditation. It's a source of the misconception that meditation or spirituality is about white-washing your mind. Most meditators feel they need to erase the "black" (bad) thoughts that arise against the "white" (good) silence and stillness, and return to whiteness. "Let's get everything white" is the source of endless frustration.

"White" provides the contrast, not the goal. The white just helps us see the black. It doesn't suggest we rub it out. But that is the suggestion most people bring to meditation. Delete those black thoughts.

Because the external is a representation of the internal (what we exhibit towards others is what we exhibit towards ourselves), this theme of erasing has monumental implications. It may seem facile and dismissive, but this is the basis for things like ethnic cleansing and the Holocaust. It's one reason we kill. As any psychologist will tell you, the problem is rarely "out there." The problem is "in here." Jews aren't the problem. Muslims aren't the problem. Americans aren't the problem. The problem is improper relationship. Don't try to rub something out. Rub in some medita-tion and realize the issue is proper relationship.

As we've seen, meditation is all about establishing a healthy relationship to thoughts and emotions. We can't establish a rela-tionship to something we can't see.

I'm not just talking about gross level thoughts, our conscious thoughts and emotions. Those are easy to see, even if you're not a meditator. Just close your eyes and that level of movement pops into view. I'm talking about subtle thoughts, those that are usually drowned out by daily activity. Below that current of subtle thought streams even more subtle currents of subconscious thoughts. In order to see these subtle and very subtle thoughts and emotions we need a good contrast medium, something that allows these movements to stand out. The meditation technique provides that medium.

Why do we want to see these subtle movements? Because they run our lives. Just because they're subconscious doesn't mean they don't affect conscious experience. It's precisely because they are so subconscious that they have so much power. It's like the cause of disease. We may not see the virus that causes an illness, let alone the DNA that is the heart of a virus, but sub-visible elements are the source of most visible disease. Our gross conscious lives are dictated by many levels of subtle subconscious elements—physical, psychological, or spiritual. As with any form of healing—physical, psychological or spiritual—if you can't identify it you'll never find a cure for it.

In terms of the psycho-spiritual, Christ powerfully proclaimed the point when he said, "Forgive them Father, for they know not what they do." Any modern psychologist would agree: our lives are driven by unseen forces. These forces include subtle thoughts and emotions. Meditation allows you to get at these, bringing subconscious triggers into the light of consciousness, and then helping you establish a conscious relationship to them. This is where the full liberating power of meditation is revealed.

Careful

If your mind does stop in meditation and all thoughts cease, this is when you need to be careful. If you don't *relate* to this experience properly it can backfire and become a trap. When your mind gets perfectly still it's almost impossible not to feel "This is it! I'm finally meditating!" The problem is that this reaction immediately sets a new standard for your meditation. You will start to measure every session against this new benchmark and you will come up short. Most of the time you will not be able to measure up because most of the time your meditation will still be full of thoughts. Your definition of meditation will shrink around this one experience, and your future meditations don't stand a chance.

This problem applies to any good meditative experience, whether it's stopping thoughts, having a super clear mind, or feeling blissed out. If you become attached to these experiences you have replaced a chain made of lead with one made of gold. Instead of being attached to your normal thoughts and emotions (the lead), you become attached to what you feel are deep meditative experiences (the gold). You're still shackled. You're chained in wanting to repeat the experience. This is a more advanced problem in meditation, but it's very common. Also, when something is deemed "good," you automatically create a new level of "bad." Once again, this is why a good definition of meditation is so important. Our traditional definitions of good and bad just don't apply to meditation.

So what should you do? Relate to the experience properly. Which means letting it go. Relate to whatever arises in your meditation with equanimity. Bliss, clarity, or non-thought are neither good nor bad. These experiences become good or bad depending on how you relate to them. Stopping your mind, or having a clear and blissful mind, is good in the sense that it points out new dimensions of experience. Aspiring for more of this mind can inspire you to practice. But there's an important difference between aspiring for something and craving for it. Aspiring is good, craving is not.

In other words, having a thought free mind is bad only if you get too attached to the experience and desperately want to repeat it. This will make you view every thought-filled meditation as now sub-standard. The one "good" experience will turn your future meditations into "bad" ones. "Non-thought" also has two meanings in meditation. The first meaning is literally having a thought free mind, but this is not as important as the second meaning. The second meaning of non-thought is not following after thoughts, or grasping at them. It's a state of healthy detachment, the witness awareness we talked about earlier. This aspect of non-thought is much more accessible, and it is good.

I'm passionate about these "feel good" traps because they've snared me for years, causing all sorts of unnecessary problems. I have also seen many other students get stuck here. In my early stages of meditation I experienced a blissful state of utter tranquility. It was a glimpse into a dimension of mind I didn't even know was possible. I desperately wanted more. On one level this inspired me to meditate more. But on another level I got really hard on myself. The majority of my meditations never reproduced that state, and that got me down. It took years to fully understand that all my meditations were just as worthy as the ones I elevated to this special status, to what I thought was "real" meditation. I heard one meditation master say, "If you've had good meditation or bad meditation, you haven't really had meditation." Real meditation is relating to whatever arises—the good, the bad, and the ugly—with equanimity.

Meet and greet

With these three phases of instruction, you're good to go. Or in this case, good to not go. You're now ready to sit. Here are a few personal tips. When I sit down to meditate I don't rush into the technique. I've found that if I take my time before I start my formal practice, and after I end it, I'm more gentle with myself and more apt to mix meditation with my day. In my early days I rushed my sessions, jammed them into my day, and started the technique the instant I sat down. Then I realized how silly it was that I was hurrying up to slow down! Over the years I've learned to blend meditation with post-meditation by easing in and out of my meditations.

Now when I meditate the first thing I do is close my eyes and feel into where I am at that moment. What's the weather like inside today? Am I sunny or cloudy? What's my mood? I don't try to change a thing, but honor where I am. I don't try to fix myself. Sometimes I feel grumpy, and give myself the space to feel grumpy. There's something authentic about touching into that without trying to change it. I'm giving myself permission to be human. I'm grumpy, so what?

I'm careful not to indulge whatever I feel, so the practice here is "touch and go." I touch into what I'm feeling, feel it fully, then let it go. I don't want touching to slip into grasping, which is usually what happens when I feel things during the day. Closing my eyes helps, because it's easier to drop into my body where my feelings— visceral or emotional—reside. What's going on in my body-mind today? Let's see (or feel) ... there's a knot in my stomach ... that's interesting ... let's touch into that for a minute. I'm feeling anxious ... how curious ... let's touch into that.

I'm not trying to be a meditator, I'm trying to be myself. I am honestly touching into who I am, and giving myself some breathing room to just be—which is another symbolic aspect of the breath phase of meditation. So after I touch into a feeling or emotion, I breathe into it. Not only am I infusing the feeling with the space of my breath, but I'm holding the feeling in that larger space. Breathing into what I'm feeling helps me keep my feelings in perspective.

Learning how to be with myself is a big deal in my meditation, and I find this prelude to my practice really helps. It's also a big deal in life. *How can I expect others to be with me when I can't even be with myself?*

Many years ago I looked deeply into my motivation in wanting to be with others, and found that it's sometimes because I wanted them to save me. But from what? I wanted people to save me from myself. There were times when I just couldn't stand myself, and being with others distracted me from this wretched loneliness, the anguish of having to be alone with my mind. With meditation, I've learned how to be alone without being lonely.

With this brief prelude to my practice, I've learned how to meet and greet myself right where I am, and to make friends with myself. By learning how to be with yourself, you may find that others like being with you more, because you're not so needy. Your natural sense of self-worth magnetizes others, who may unknowingly seek the same qualities you now embody.

You may also discover that it's easier for you to be with others. This is because when you touch into your feelings you're touching into the feelings of everyone on this planet. You're connecting to them, and getting to know them at a deep level. Everyone knows what pain, joy, sadness, and fear feels like. Touch into yourself and you will touch others. Friendships abound when you learn how to make friends with yourself.

Contemplation – Driven to distraction

Why do you impulsively fill your days with activity? Why the rush to always turn on the TV, check your phone, or run to your computer? Many of us are almost desperate not to be left alone with ourselves—we're scared to be alone with our mind. I'm not talking about having an evening away from your family to relax or read a book, but having an entire evening alone with your mind—with absolutely no distractions. Would being alone with your mind drive you nuts? Prisoners in solitary confinement rage against the loneliness, the torture of being so alone with themselves. Veteran meditators crave for that same solitude, and delight in being with themselves. Distraction and discontent are virtually synonymous.

Being alone with your mind will not drive you clinically crazy, but it does drive you into distraction—a more subtle form of craziness. When you're afraid of being alone with your mind (think about meditating all day long) what are you afraid of? Are you afraid of what you don't know? Get to know your mind, make pals with it, and fear is replaced with friendship.

Some days when I meditate I meet the irritable Andrew and chuckle, "Hello Mr. Cranky, how are you today? Crabby? Okay, let's feel it fully." Other times I feel blissful, and feel into that. I try to relate to the highs and lows without preference. It's not easy, equanimity is part of my practice, but after years of doing this I've become more level headed because I practice it.

Like you, I have a colorful array of feelings, and as unique as those feelings are to me, they're not that special—nor am I. The feelings also keep recycling, the same feeling with a different story line, but they're only as special as I make them. Because I've greeted all these aspects of myself so many times, they no longer have as much power over me. They're like mental waves that crash over my body as I sit. I continue to feel them as they wash over me, in fact I feel them more than ever because I'm so open to them, but like a big rock on the shore they no longer move me. Because I'm unmoved doesn't mean I'm untouched, or less human. Since I give myself the space to feel so much more, and do so honestly, I feel like I'm more human—but less neurotic.

I do my meditative prelude for a few minutes, always careful not to indulge or judge what I feel, then open my eyes, lower my gaze, and begin the technique.

At the end of my practice I do a short coda before getting up. Since I'm a musician, I like these musical analogies. The coda is to slowly start moving my limbs, to look around, and to touch back into what I'm feeling now. The movement prepares me for getting up and starting my day, and touching back into what I'm feeling recapitulates the theme of staying in contact with myself, and staying friendly. Because I've greeted myself properly, I'm now ready to meet and greet you.

My meditations are like a sonata for my soul. There's the prelude, the main theme (which is the technique), all the variations and improvisations that unfold during my session, and then the coda. There's no finale per se, because I don't want to end my meditation as I move into the world. The finale, if there is one, is taking my practice with me and sharing it with you.

When I sit in meditation I'm playing out the symphony of my being, celebrating every sound. Every session is different, so the music of my mind is constantly changing. The performance occurs in post-meditation, when I take what I've learned on the cushion and spread it onto the stage of my life. But the point is this: my life isn't just noise anymore. By making friends with myself I'm in harmony with my being, and therefore more in tune with you. And because I've seen the same melodies of thought, the same dissonance of conflicting emotions, the same variations on a fundamental theme (of being human) countless times—I've become more composed.

Conclusion

These three phases of body, speech, and mind create that stable tripod, the "stand" of your meditation. The further you go with your meditation the more you'll discover how each phase of instruction applies to the others, and how they all work to bootstrap your practice. In other words, these three phases lift each other up. When you're doing your practice, keep the basic instructions simple. Refer to just the opening paragraphs of these last three chapters. When you want to go deeper, you can supplement your own discoveries with the commentary that surrounds these basic instructions. There is a lifetime of discovery awaiting you.

CHAPTER 9

How Do I Keep Going?

A s with any new discipline, a big challenge in meditation is maintaining it. It's easy to be inspired at first. Meditation is new, exotic, and almost fashionable. But like any new diet or exercise fad, sooner or later the inspiration fades. It's like falling in love. Sooner or later you fall out of love and into reality. The romance dwindles and the work of mature love begins. The honeymoon always ends.

There are a number of things you can do to sustain your practice. First, use your inspiration to get the ball rolling. It does take an initial push, so use your enthusiasm to make that push. If you establish enough momentum up front, meditation will start to "do you." It will carry you. Remember that most of the effort comes at the beginning, during the first phase of mindfulness called effortful mindfulness. This is the manual labor phase.

How long you spend at this first phase depends on the quality and quantity of your practice. If you're seriously into it and practice consistently and whole-heartedly, the fruits of effortful mindfulness are picked quickly. If you dabble at meditation you'll never get to the second phase. There's nothing wrong with staying at the level of effortful mindfulness. It's still a wonderful stage of practice. But the natural and spontaneous "performance" of mindfulness doesn't arise without practice.

After some time, this phase matures into effortless mindfulness. This is when mindfulness takes on a life of its own and becomes increasingly spontaneous. It starts to pop up more frequently until it eventually stays up. But to reach this point you have to keep it up. You have to counteract all the mindlessness with your practice of mindfulness. It's like turning around the Titanic that's been cruising on full throttle across the Atlantic. There's so much mindless momentum that pulling the U-turn into mindfulness takes time. So be patient. Realize that your proficiency in mindlessness is the result of your nearly constant practice of it. I was at a retreat recently where one funny participant, probably speaking on behalf of most meditators, said, "Come on inner peace, I ain't got all day!"

Let's say you're fifty years old and decide to start practicing meditation for twenty minutes a day. For fun, let's do the math. If you're awake for sixteen hours a day, that's 960 minutes a day. Multiply that times 365 days and you get 350,000 minutes a year. Multiply that times 50 years and you get 17,520,000 minutes. How is 20 minutes of mindfulness (and how much of that 20 minutes is really mindful?) going to stand up against 17,520,000 minutes of mindlessness? Which state of mind are you more familiar with? You get the idea. This isn't meant to discourage you, or make you feel that meditation will never turn the tide, but to simply be realistic about your expectations. Meditation isn't minute-made. Practicing twenty minutes a day does change people, but it doesn't change them overnight.

Because we're so habituated into mindlessness, we're naturally mindless. But as we've seen, we didn't get that way naturally. We unknowingly worked at it. Because of all our training, mindlessness is now our default. It's where we automatically go. With practice we can get flip the tables and get to the point where we default into mindfulness. We can replace, "I can't help it, I'm always distracted," with "I can't help it, I'm always mindful."

As our companion book (*Fire and Ice; On the Benefits of Meditation*) shows, beneficial things are happening even if they're not initially visible. Studies have shown that you literally re-wire your brain when you meditate—whether you know it or not.[24] The changes are initially subtle, but they become gradually more apparent. You will begin to notice the changes, or others might comment on them. Having faith in the practice, and the science that supports it, helps you stick with it.

It's also important to realize that meditation is not a linear process. While mindfulness does evolve over months and years, it doesn't do so in a straightforward fashion. You might have the greatest meditation one day, only to sit down the next day and feel like you've never meditated. Meditation is like the stock market, up one day and down the next. The key to a successful investment is not to get elated by the highs and depressed by the lows. Ride the fluctuating market of your mind with equanimity, and you will be rewarded for your investment of patience and perseverance. And once again, because meditation is not linear, the criteria for success is different than for most other things.

The nuts and bolts of habit

To establish the good habit of mindfulness let's look at the mechanics of habit itself. Habits rule our lives. On one level, you are what you repeatedly do. When a habit is fully ingrained, it "does" you. A habit can take on such force that we simply can't help

---

24 See *Train Your Mind Change Your Brain: How a New Science Reveals Our Extraordinary Potential to Transform Ourselves,* by Sharon Begley, Ballantine Books, New York, NY, 2008.

ourselves, as any smoker or drug addict can attest. When properly harnessed, however, we can use the power of habit in our favor so that meditation eventually "does us," as any meditation master can attest.

Habit itself is neutral. It's inherently neither good nor bad. What we want to do is use the force of habit to shape a good one. Studies have shown that it takes from 18 to 254 days for a habit to take root.[25] During that time you simply have to do it. But don't over do it. If you try too hard you can flame out. Use your inspiration to ignite and fan the spark, but be careful not to blow it out.

The meditative path is also not the same from one person to the next, so be careful not to compare yourself to others. You can use others to lift you up, but be careful not to let them take you down. If a meditating friend is red hot on their path, and you're lukewarm, that might discourage you. Everyone has their own path. While there are many similarities in the stages of meditation, everyone traverses those stages differently. Trust your path, believe in yourself, and be realistic. The mind is always becoming more and more familiar, and therefore more proficient, with either mindfulness or mindlessness. If you're mindless fifteen out of the sixteen hours of your day, it's not realistic to expect your one hour of mindfulness to counteract the other fifteen.

In the late 1970's, psychologists James Prochaska and Carlo DiClemente came up with a five-stage model for change. It was devised to help people stop smoking, but the principles apply to any level of habituation.

Stage One: Pre-contemplation, or "I'm not ready to change." This is the "ignorance is bliss" stage, and where most people are. In regards to meditation, you're unaware that your behavior (mindlessness) is causing any problems. You may have heard that

---

25 See *How Habits are Formed: Modeling habit formation in the real world*, by Phillippa Lally, Cornelia H. M. van Jaarsveld, Henry W. W. Potts, and Jane Wardle, in the European Journal of Social Psychology, Volume 49, Issue 6, p. 998-1009, October 2010.

mindfulness is beneficial, but you're not interested. You're cozy in your bad unconscious habits. There's no motivation to change because you're not aware that there's a problem—or an opportunity. You would never pick up a book like this.

How to work through it: Be aware of this stage. Then realize that your mindlessness will only get worse and cause even more unrest. As we saw in Chapter One, without a proper diagnosis there'll never be a cure. Ignorance is not bliss. Awareness is bliss. Look at the effects of rampant mindless in your life and in the world.

Stage Two: Contemplating change. This is the "I'm sitting on the fence" stage. You're considering the change, looking at the pros and cons of meditation, starting to contemplate the benefits. Maybe you've had a wake up call, the realization that you're too speedy and stressed. You're not meditating yet, but you think it might be a good idea. You're ready to buy this book.

To evolve to the next level: Learn more about the benefits of meditation. Contemplate your life; look at the damaging effects of mindlessness. Think about how your life will be if you don't change. There'll be more stress, distraction, and dis-ease. Maybe even an ulcer or a breakdown. Then contemplate how your life might look if you do start to meditate. Use the power of mental imagery, or visualization, to see yourself peaceful and happy. Create an image of a calmer and happier you.

Stage Three: Preparing to change, to take action. This is the "I'm testing the waters" stage. You're ready to take small steps towards actually meditating. You build momentum by setting small goals. You're reading about meditation, ready to take a class, and maybe buy a meditation cushion. You're going to go to that meditation center.

To evolve to the next level: Talk to people who meditate. Find a meditation instructor. Invest in the props. Put your money where your mouth is.

Stage Four: Changing, taking action. This is the "I'm finally doing it" phase. You're actually meditating. Congratulations. You've crossed the threshold into action, now the trick is sustaining it. Because the new habit is not fully established you can still relapse. Some researchers say this phase lasts three to six months. To get to this 4th stage, real time and effort has been invested. You're now into it.

To evolve to the next level: Celebrate your efforts and your success at reaching this stage. You're actually meditating! Continue to meditate, read books, take classes, and find like-minded friends. Deepen your relationship with meditation instruction.

Stage Five: Maintenance, keeping up the good habit. This is the "I really want to keep this up" phase. After six months of sustained change, you've probably reached the maintenance phase. Just like with any discipline you can always slip back, but good momentum has been established. The habit has been formed and meditation can start to carry you.

To maintain this level: reflect upon and implement everything in this book.

Everyone is different and every habit is different. It's a lot easier to start flossing than it is to start meditating. The more ingrained a bad habit becomes, like smoking or being mindless, the harder it is to supplant it with a good one. Some people create good habits easily, others really struggle. The point is to focus on your good habit day to day, and don't worry about how long it takes. The journey is the goal.

The power of view

Many meditation masters assert that if you're having problems getting to the cushion, it's because your view isn't strong enough. View is a word that refers to your understanding of meditation—its benefits, the philosophy behind it, everything we're doing in this book. I like this term because it denotes a sense of clear vision. You see the benefits of meditation and where it can take you.

View is the first part of a three-part progression that defines the entire path of meditation. The other two parts are meditation and action. View, meditation, and action form the structure of this book. We started with the view, describing what meditation is and why it's so helpful. We then progressed into meditation instruction. In the final chapters we will discuss the fruits of view and meditation in terms of action, or how to apply meditation to life.

Each of these three phases builds on its predecessor. If you don't have a good foundation with your view, you don't know what you're doing or where you're going with your meditation. You stumble this way and that, getting lost in all sorts of detours or dead ends. There's no sense of path. Without a good view where is this path going? This can eventually cause people to stop meditating. But with a strong view, meditation naturally follows. You get it. You know where you're going. When your meditation is strong, the final aspect of action also happens naturally. You spontaneously start to act from a meditative point of view.

So to really strengthen and sustain your meditation, strengthen your view. Read books, take seminars, talk to meditators. Learn as much as you can about the power of meditation and that power will propel you onto the cushion.

Think about death

Most people don't like to think about death, or any end-of-life matters. But in my life, thinking about old age and death has helped me more than anything. Nothing puts things in perspective more quickly. I sometimes imagine lying on my deathbed, reflecting on my life. What has given me the greatest meaning? What was a waste of time? Where did I stray? Then I take those reflections and apply them now.

This may not work for everybody, because most people prefer to live in the denial of death. But these reflections are a powerful way to show you what's truly important. When I look back on my life, there are a number of things I regret and mistakes I have certainly made. But the one thing I never regret is the time I spent in meditation. My retreats were not a mistake, despite some of the hardships. My daily meditations were not a waste, despite the hassles. Sure, I loved the vacations to Switzerland or the Caribbean, but what has brought me the deepest satisfaction, and sense of meaning, is my meditation. This is where I feel the most genuine and alive. This is where I feel I'm not wasting this precious life. My meditation isn't always easy, but it is always meaningful.

So I take these reflections and use them to inspire me to meditate now. They also help me prune away frivolous activity. Without contemplations of this sort, it's so easy to slip into complacency or laziness. With so many distractions, it's so easy to waste hours, days, weeks—or an entire life. In the spiritual traditions, reflecting on impermanence and death has always been a potent way to spur people into meaningful activity. Think about it.

Supernatural help

For those who have a connection to higher powers, like God, Krishna, Christ, Mohammed, or the Buddha, or to unseen beings like angels, spirits, or deities, prayer is an effective aid. Because of my scientific background, I used to dismiss this supernatural stuff. If you can't see it, it doesn't exist. But after forty years on my meditative and spiritual path, I am now a believer. I now realize that I am not alone, and that I can call upon "energies" to help me. It seems naïve, even arrogant, not to acknowledge the existence of higher forces.

It doesn't matter what you call it—energies, deities, messengers, protectors, or guardian angels. What matters, if you believe in this, is establishing a relationship to these energies and asking for their help. You can do this via ritual, prayer, or supplication. At the end of my meditations, I make a heartfelt prayer to my protectors to keep me from falling into distraction, and to help me stay on my path. I know how hard it is to keep meditating, and the incredible force of bad habit and distraction. I'm not shy to ask for help anywhere I can get it.

For me, the secret is to really cry out for help, from the bottom of my heart. If I just pay lip service to my request, not much happens. But when I really mean it, things happen that help me stay on track. It's often subtle and always "anonymous." In other words, you could rationalize the effects in more scientific terms, or dismiss them as mere coincidence. I can't explain how it works, but it does. Anyone who has felt the force of prayer knows that something is going on. It's magical, and I'm okay with magic.

Like with the death contemplation, the supplication for supernatural help may not be for everyone. For me, it's no longer supernatural. It's just natural.

Not just for me

When I'm struggling to get to the meditation cushion, I'll often think about others. I think about my family and friends, those I work with, and even the strangers I'll meet. This helps me get out of myself, and to think bigger. I try to remember that I'm not just meditating for myself. I'm meditating to become a better person for others.

This transforms my laziness, and helps me go to "work" for others. It's like a parent going to work to support their family. They may not want to get out of bed and head to the office, but they do so because they want to care for their family. So when I get lazy I approach my meditation with this attitude: even though it's a hassle, I'm going to meditate in order to help others.

It may seem contrived but it works for me. I'm going to nurture this good habit of meditation because it helps me be a good person. I want to be more patient, understanding, and compassionate so that when I meet you I can be there for you.

Fresh start

"Fresh start" is important in meditation. We tend to beat ourselves up in meditation because of all the history we bring to it. We may already have undercurrents of thought that tug us down, "I'm a loser. I can't do anything meaningful. I can't meditate." These thoughts, our personal history, can infect our meditation. History has its place in the classroom, not in our meditation room. The great writer James Joyce once said, "History is a nightmare from which I am trying to awake." Meditation is about the present, not the past, and this present is always fresh. That's what we want to wake up to.

Scientists and sages describe reality as the moment-to-moment arising and dissolving of everything. Physicists tell us that sub-atomic particles pop in and out of existence at dizzying velocities. Every experience of the physical world of matter is therefore fresh. Mystics tell us that consciousness pops in and out of existence at inconceivable frequencies. Every experience of the mental world is also fresh. If we connect to that freshness we can refresh our meditation.

Meditation can get stale. Do anything long enough and it can get stale. "Fresh start" ventilates that stuffiness. This is how to practice it: when you're sitting in meditation and nothing seems to be working, or the fizzle is gone, just drop the whole thing. Hit your restart button. Collapse your posture, look out the window, and release everything for a few moments. Take a few deep breaths, stretch your legs, stand up, or do whatever you need to energize your practice. Then start again.

I have done this countless times to amp up my practice. It's like opening the window in a stuffy room. Sometimes my break lasts a few seconds, other times a few minutes. If I return to sitting and don't feel refreshed, I just stop. You want to end your sessions when meditation still feels good. That will help you return to it. If you grind it out you won't enjoy meditation, and will probably quit. Don't turn your meditation into a marathon. Keep it crisp and alive.

The place where you can extend your sessions, and gently challenge yourself, is in group meditation. See what it's like to practice beyond your comfort zone. Feel into the stretch. Let the support of those sitting with you inspire you. Notice the benefits of healthy "peer pressure." Do you learn new things about yourself when you practice longer? What's your resistance to longer sessions? Explore your mind, and make friends with it, during these longer sessions. However, always be gentle to yourself. Don't turn a healthy stretch into a hurtful strain.

"Fresh start" also applies at a bigger level, and here we have to be careful. If you feel like your meditation altogether isn't clicking or just feels flat, it's okay to take a break. Remember that meditation is about developing kindness towards yourself. If you're fighting it what's the point? Take some time off. Then return with a fresh start.

The reason we have to be careful is because it's so easy to drift away forever. The force of distraction is enormous, on the cushion and in life. Entertainment and comfort rule our lives, and meditation isn't always entertaining or comfortable. If you're not careful, before you know it months or years have gone by. So if you feel the need to take a longer break, talk to a meditation instructor. Stay connected with your meditation friends. This is when it's good to check your motivation. Are you taking a healthy break, or running away? Are you caving in to comfort, or honestly needing to pause?

Ego is very clever. It will tempt you in every possible way to keep you from meditating. It will whisper, "You have better things to do. You're too busy. Meditation is a waste of time. You knew you couldn't do it." So be aware of these devilish distractions. In meditation we're always tuning the instrument of our mind. Like a violin, if it's too tight the string will snap. If it's too lose the string will sag. The music of meditation resounds as we continually go "sharp" or "flat" with our practice, and adjust it accordingly. Ups and downs are part of any aspect of life. Fine-tuning is the name of this game, and "fresh start" is one of the best ways to play it.

Gray is beautiful

Be careful to avoid back and white thinking. This is when there's either success or failure, I'm doing it or I'm not, and nothing in between. In meditation, gray is gorgeous. Fuzzy is fantastic. That's where meditation happens. Don't trap yourself with images of success or failure. Like meditation itself, definitions of success or failure are wide open. If you're looking for success in meditation, start by having good definitions of both. In this regard, meditation isn't like anything else. You can't judge your successes and failures using conventional standards.

Who is the successful meditator? One who does it. The journey of meditation is the success story. Rain or shine, good days and bad, the successful meditator returns to their cushion with gentle and humorous determination.

Who is a failed meditator? One who loses heart. This usually means someone with a failed definition of meditation, or who probably set the bar too high. It's really hard to fail at meditation. What can fail, and this is good, are your limited definitions. These failures are actually successes because they help you refine your understanding. On one level, the only real failure is simply not meditating.

Miscellaneous tips

I've been playing the piano since I was five years old, and one of the best tips to get me to practice over all these years is also a good one that has gotten me to meditate. It's called *The Ten Minute Rule,* and many music teachers use it. When you don't feel like practicing, tell yourself you're just going to do it for ten minutes. More often than not, after ten minutes you'll find yourself practicing more. Getting to the piano bench, or the meditation cushion, is usually the hardest part. Once you're there it's generally easy to keep going. You're kind of tricking yourself, but it works.

There are times when ten minutes is all I can do, but most of the time I keep going. I've heard yoga instructors share a similar tip. When you don't feel like doing a full session of yoga, just do one Sun Salutation, which takes about 45 seconds. That often leads to two, then three, and before you know it you're into a full session. Take a small bite and you'll often eat the whole meal.

Here are a handful of other tips, not necessarily in order of priority, that can help you keep going.

- Be kind to yourself. Meditation is new and different. It can feel awkward till you get the hang of it. Have a sense of humor and be patient.
- Start small. Meditate ten to twenty minutes a day at first. Ease into it and see how it feels. Don't set the bar too high.
- Build on small success. You've done your first session, that's great. You practiced five days in a row! Terrific.
- Use the props. Refer back to Chapter Five for all the helpful supports.
- Be aware of negative self-talk. Everybody criticizes themselves at first. Be aware of this tendency and smile at it. "I'm hopeless as a meditator," "I knew I couldn't do it," the list is endless. Let these thoughts come and let them go.
- Allow for imperfection. You're human, and therefore wonderfully imperfect. Join the club. Striving for perfection is demoralizing. You will never be your version of a perfect meditator. Be yourself. That's the perfect version.
- Tell other people you're meditating. It creates healthy peer support, and holds you accountable in a light way.
- Write down your goals, for example to try meditation for twenty-one days. There's something powerful about putting your intentions on paper.
- Meditate first thing in the morning and try to do it the same time and place. Routine is habit-forming. The more consistent you are with time and place the more rapidly the habit takes form. Doing it before you get going is always helpful.
- Find like-minded friends who meditate. This creates informal support groups that are very helpful. If it feels

right, join a community of meditators. The power of positive peer support cannot be overstated.

- Attend meditation programs and do group retreats. Do a daylong program, or a weekend. Read books, check out meditation websites and chat rooms. The more you soak in this material the more inspired you will get.
- Hang around meditation masters, or veteran meditators. It's inspiring to be around those who have been practicing for decades. You can see how it affects everything they do. Real meditation masters are humble, so be careful not to let the marketing skills of the pseudo masters seduce you.

CHAPTER 10

Extending Meditation Into Life

Meditation is a wonderful practice in its own right. But formal meditation itself isn't the final point. If you get fixated on formal practice, meditation won't reach into the rest of your life. The qualities of the heart and mind that are developed in meditation, and that then perfume your every day life, are the point. Remember the progression of view into meditation into action. Mindful action, life itself, is the final stage. The fruition, and the best way to evaluate the success of your practice, is what meditation does for the rest of your life. As we've seen, the measure of meditation is not just how mindful you are when you sit, but how mindful you are during the day. It's not how pacified you are when you practice, but how peacefully you can handle the difficulties in life.

One of the biggest mistakes is to think that meditation is just what you do on your cushion. You start there, but then the benefits expand. Your formal sessions are like a container where you nurture the essentials, but this container is full of holes. It leaks, and meditation starts to saturate your life.

Just like any discipline, the effects are initially subtle. A few months after I started meditating I was driving to meet a friend. An aggressive driver cut me off, forcing me to slam on the brakes. As my heart pounded from this near accident, I realized I didn't fall into my usual response of hitting the horn, or making an obscene gesture. I didn't take the event personally, and was less reactive. This was one of the first signs that something was changing.

Meditation naturally extends into life, but there are things you can do to help. Even though sitting meditation is the best posture for practice, in the classic texts there are three other formal ways to meditate. The first is walking meditation. Many meditation centers mix sessions of sitting with short sessions of walking. People tend to view walking meditation as a break from practice, but it's actually a way to extend practice. On one level it is a break, or at least a change, from sitting. But it's not a break from being mindful. You can also use walking meditation as a way to "downshift" into sitting. In other words, you could do a brief walking meditation as a way to transition from daily life into your sitting practice.

In walking meditation the emphasis shifts from being mindful of your breath to being mindful of your movement. Bring your awareness to the sensation of your feet touching the ground, the natural movement of walking, and the space around you. When a thought or other distraction arises, you don't have to label it "thinking." Notice that you've strayed and return to your walking.

To bring a sense of practice to your walking, several things help. First, walk slowly. You're transitioning from the stillness of sitting to the busyness of daily life, and slowness is a good way to do that. Second, instead of letting your arms swing back and forth as in normal walking, assume this hand posture: wrap the fingers of your left hand around your thumb in the "fist of non-aggression," hold that fist gently against your navel, and then cradle that fist with your right hand.

If you're meditating at home, you can do a three to five minute walking meditation for every twenty minutes or so of sitting. Get up slowly, and then walk around the room in a clockwise direction. Then return to your cushion and resume sitting.

The other two classic postures, standing and lying down, are not as commonly practiced. Experiment with these two postures and see if they work for you. Sometimes sitting meditation is called the "middle way posture" between standing and lying down. In this regard, standing would be "too tight" and lying down would be "too loose." But it's good to play with all three, and see how these postures affect your mind.

With standing meditation, make sure your posture is straight. Not quite military stiff, but upright. It's good to do this in front of a mirror at first, or to have someone correct your stand. We tend to slouch our shoulders or droop our head, so tuck your head in above your spinal column, bring your shoulders back, and expose your heart. Your arms can hang naturally at your side, or with palms turned forward. Pay attention to your feet on the ground, the sense of gravity, and the space around you. When your mind strays, gently bring it back without labeling. Stand for a few minutes, then sit back down. Notice what this "too tight" posture does to your mind. Are you more attentive (like the military command to stand at "ATTENTION!") or distracted? Dullness often has a physical aspect. So if your mind is heavy when you sit, try standing up for a few minutes.

With the lying down posture, lie on your back, with your hands gently resting on your belly. Keep your eyes open. Once again, the middle way approach even applies to this posture. Lying down on a hard floor is too tight; lying down on a soft bed is too loose. Lying down on a rug, yoga mat, or a few meditation pads is ideal.

Bring your awareness to the sensation of your body on the ground, and the movement of your breath. When your mind strays, bring it back to your body and breath. Because we associate lying down with sleep, notice how this "too loose" posture affects your mind. Are you groggier lying down? Is it harder to stay awake?

Again, most meditators just sit, or sit and walk during formal meditation sessions. But it's good to mix it up. Expand your sense of practice. See how these postures affect your mind, but be careful not to get discursive in the postures. In other words, don't switch from one posture to another just because you're bored. I recommend choosing just one other posture in addition to sitting, and experiment with it. It doesn't have to be part of your daily practice.

If you only associate meditation with sitting, it's harder to extend your meditation into life. By practicing in these other postures you're spreading your sense of meditation. The next time you're standing in line at the checkout counter, you might suddenly click into a meditative mind because of your history of formal standing meditation. When you walk across the parking lot, you might remember your walking meditation and bring mindfulness to your gait. When you lie down to sleep, you might become more settled because of your formal practice of lying down meditation.

At the end of each session, get up slowly. Take a few moments to transition from meditation to post-meditation. This helps you extend the "mood" of meditation. If you leap up and rush off to breakfast, you will probably leap away from your mindfulness. Take your time. Stretch your legs, or mindfully look around before getting up. Notice how quickly physical movement invites mental movement (more thoughts), and how easy it is to lose your meditative mind. When I make the transition from meditation to post-meditation, I tighten my mindfulness and use that as a springboard to launch me, mindfully, into life.

Short sessions repeated frequently

Short sessions repeated frequently are another way to expand meditation. Some people feel that short sessions aren't worth the trouble, that only longer meditations really work. But short sessions are incredibly helpful.

What constitutes a short session? That's up to you. It can be as short as a flash of mindfulness, a few seconds of being mindful, or a few minutes. It doesn't matter. What matters is that you start to sprinkle meditation onto everything. Some meditative traditions talk about the experience of "one taste," how it is that everything starts to taste like meditation. Spicing up your life with mindfulness and awareness is a fantastic thing. So whenever you can, remember to flash mindfulness onto the present moment. The essence of meditative practice is remembrance, and mindfulness, (drenpa, or "recollection" in Tibetan), is its fundamental expression.

Here's an image that helps. Most meditation centers have meditation gongs. These gongs are struck as a way to signal the start and end of group practice. I think of flashing onto mindfulness as "hitting the gong of mindfulness." In other words, I "hit" the moment with my mindfulness and then rest in the reverberation of being present. I don't keep hitting the gong over and over, saying something like "I must be mindful! I must be mindful!" That's too tight. I just strike the moment with my awareness, and then let it go. In this way I mindfully "hum" throughout the day.

What constitutes frequent sessions? That's also up to you. If you have a watch that can be set to beep every hour, train yourself to associate that beep with a flash of mindfulness. You can also associate other activities, like brushing your teeth or washing dishes, with mindfulness. Use your imagination and see what works for you. Muslims do brief prayers (Salah) five times a day. That's a nice way for them to stay connected to their faith. But don't set the bar too high, saying for example, "I'm going to be mindful 100 times each day!" That could lead to frustration. Great expectations should be replaced with reasonable aspirations.

Meditation masters often say that beginners should practice in short sessions, maybe five or ten minutes, then take a short break of a minute or so. During the break you can relax the method, but not the sense of mindfulness. This is a great way to practice extending meditation into life. Sogyal Rinpoche is one of those masters: "Sometimes when you have been struggling to practice, curiously, the very moment when you take a break from the method—if you are still mindful and present—is the moment when meditation actually happens. That is why the break is just as important a part of meditation as the sitting itself. Sometimes I tell my students who are having problems with their practice to practice during the break and take a break during their meditation!"[26]

In your meditation sessions, effort is obviously involved, but the idea is to relax. In your post-meditation, which is where we tend to flop back into mindlessness, the idea is to gently tighten up. Sharpen your mindfulness and exert some more effort to keep you from being distracted. With our theme of not too tight and not too loose, you can be a little loose in your meditation and a little tight in your post-meditation. This helps you blend the two so that eventually everything becomes your meditation. In other words, you're naturally mindful all the time.

While sitting meditation is obviously important, far more important is your state of mind after formal practice. A calm and collected mind—a meditative mind—is what you want to extend into life. Here's a Zen story that illustrates this:

> "Master, how do you put enlightenment into action? How do you practice it in everyday life?" asked the student.

---

26 See *Glimpse After Glimpse, Daily Reflections on Living and Dying*, by Sogyal Rinpoche, HarperOne, New York, NY, 1995, April 28 entry.

"By eating and by sleeping," replied the master.

"But Master, everybody sleeps and eats."

"But not everybody eats when they eat, or sleeps when they sleep," said the master.

From this comes the famous Zen saying: "When I eat, I eat; when I sleep, I sleep." This means being fully present while eating or sleeping, or in anything you do. Most of us don't eat when we eat. Our body may be eating, but our mind is usually feasting on some thought or fantasy.

Don't underestimate the power of short frequent sessions. They add up. The scholar Huston Smith said that the process of the meditative path is to transform flashes of illumination into abiding light. Keep flashing (remembering) your mindfulness and it will get to the point where the light of awareness is always on. You never forget. That's when effortful mindfulness matures into effortless mindfulness. That's when meditation starts to "do" you.

Once you understand what meditation is, you can practice it anywhere at anytime. That's the point. Mindfulness and awareness applies to anything, not just sitting. There's eating meditation, driving meditation, showering meditation, cooking meditation ... the list is endless. The spirit behind all these additional methods (walking, standing, lying down, short sessions) is not to let your formal sessions restrict your sense of meditation. Let your life become your meditation.

Contemplation - Come to your senses

If I were to ask you right now to meditate, what would that mean? What would you shift to transform this moment into meditation? What constitutes the meditative mind? You would probably stop reading, settle your mind, and focus on what's happening with your senses. You would pay attention to the present moment, not the thoughts or emotions flowing through your mind. What do you hear? What do you smell, feel, or see? You would come to your senses—literally and figuratively. So use your senses, which can only function in the present moment, to connect your wandering mind to the present moment. It's so sensible and simple.

Sogyal Rinpoche again:

Sit for a short time; then take a break, a very short break of about thirty seconds or a minute. But be mindful of whatever you do, and do not lose your presence and its natural ease. Then alert yourself and sit again. If you do many short sessions like this, your breaks will often make your meditation more real and more inspiring; they will take the clumsy, irksome rigidity, solemnity, and unnaturalness out of your practice and bring you more and more focus and ease. Gradually, through this interplay of breaks and sitting, the barrier between meditation and everyday life will crumble, the contrast between them will dissolve, and you will find yourself increasingly in your natural pure presence, without distraction. Then, as Dudjom Rinpoche used to say: "Even though the meditator may leave the meditation, the meditation will not leave the meditator.[27]

Spontaneous expressions

Even if you don't do these supplemental practices, meditation will start to expand. This is because meditation works with your mind, and your mind is involved with everything you do. When you get up from a meditation session you don't just leave your

27 See *Glimpse After Glimpse, Daily Reflections on Living and Dying,* by Sogyal Rinpoche, HarperOne, New York, NY, 1995, June 13 entry.

mind behind on the cushion. You may leave your mindfulness behind, but it will eventually catch up to you. When it does, which happens with more and more meditation practice, you will find yourself spontaneously more mindful. You will find that all the qualities of mind and heart that you've developed in your meditation sessions start to follow you, like a shadow of wisdom. They start to become you—in both senses of that phrase.

CHAPTER 11

Common Traps, Challenges, and Remedies

A s with any discipline, there are traps that can snare the unsuspecting meditator. Knowing about them can help you anticipate the pitfalls and remedy the problems. We've already addressed some of the most common ones, like feeling that you're a bad meditator, or that you just can't do it. As we've seen, this usually happens because the bar has been set too high with your faulty definition. So the first remedy for a host of problems is to have a good definition of meditation.

Discouragement is very common. Meditation is like the evolution of a relationship between lovers. The romance fades, and is replaced with the challenges of sustaining mature love. But with the work comes the rewards. Discouragement often comes from expecting too much too fast. Be patient and realistic. You can't learn to play the piano in a month and you won't see the effects of meditation right away. In the Taoist tradition there's a story about a new farmer who just couldn't wait for his crops to grow. In his impatience he went to the field and tugged on the plants to make them grow faster, which of course only uprooted them. Impatience can uproot any meditation.

In this age of instant gratification, patience and discipline are like unused muscles shriveling away. These are exactly the muscles required for meditation. When you exercise them with your meditation practice they get stronger, and so does your meditation. Patience and discipline are simultaneously the requirements, and the fruits, of any practice.

Meditators often complain that they're not making any progress. Once again, this depends on how you define progress. In the world of meditation, there's a different set of criteria for progress. For example, studies have shown that meditation increases sadness.[28] From a conventional point of view this is hardly progress. We want to be happy, not sad. But remember that sadness in its truest sense means "having enough, being sated." With meditation, you realize that the fullness of the present moment is all you need to be happy. You're satisfied with just being here now.

Secondly, progress depends on what you're actually doing when you meditate. If you're just hanging out daydreaming or lost in thought on the cushion, nothing will change. You may stay out of trouble, but you will not become mindful. Meditators have to be honest with themselves, always on the lookout for self-deception. Just because you're sitting doesn't mean you're doing sitting meditation. It's easy to fool yourself, which is why a meditation instructor is so helpful. They keep your practice honest.

Think about the first phase of meditation as laying down the roots. As you sit on the cushion you're planting the roots of a majestic redwood. Every time you sit, the roots are watered and grow deeper. When the roots mature, the trunk develops, and from that the branches and the leaves.

---

28 Reported by Clifford Saron, lead scientist in the Shamatha Project (a study on meditation), in a presentation at the Mind and Life Symposium, April 2012, Denver, Colorado.

How long does this take? It depends on the quality and quantity of your practice. Studies show that changes can occur in as little as eight weeks, and with as little as twelve minutes a day of practice.[29] But again, don't let this data create expectations. Just do the practice for its own sake and find out what works for you.

So in terms of discouragement, it's okay to have expectations, just be reasonable. In this modern age we want results—and fast. Slow and steady are key ingredients in meditation. If you follow the technique and practice regularly, you will see results. Millions of meditators across thousands of years guarantee it.

Boredom is common and frequently derails a meditator. In this age we've replaced the threat of boredom with the burden of busyness. There are two phases of boredom in meditation. The first is called "hot boredom." This is when the monotony of meditation makes you want to jump out of your skin. You start squirming and suddenly have to check your email, or text messages. You must return that call. In these instances, remind yourself that if your response is so important, it will still be important when you finish your practice. Hot boredom tends to arise in longer group sessions, when there's more pressure to hang in there. The mindless mind isn't just hungry for distraction. It's starving.

This is when you need to smile and realize how good you've become at being mindless. You're just reaping the fruits of all your mindless practice. Everybody goes through it. It may not be comfortable, but it's natural. Be kind to yourself, realize that it's just your mind ravenous for entertainment, and then make friends with the boredom. Establish a relationship to it. It won't kill you.

If you don't meditate with a group or don't stretch yourself past your comfort zone, a solitary meditator often stops practicing

---

29 See *Mindfulness Meditation Training Changes Brain Structure in Eight Weeks*, in the online magazine *Science Daily*, Jan 21, 2011. See *Meditate for Just 12 Minutes a Day to Prevent Memory Loss*, by Mehmet C. Oz, and Michael F. Roizen, in the online magazine *Real Age*, April 6, 2012.

when they get bored. So if you only practice alone, every once in awhile gently push yourself till you do get bored, or at least hold yourself to the time you set for yourself without stopping early. Remember that stretching, in any discipline, is good for growth.

If you continue past this hot phase, it will mature into cool boredom. You still feel the pangs to move, but they no longer have as much power. You're bored, so what? You're starting to chill out. Cool boredom is therefore a sign of progress. You're finally quelling the fires of inflammation.

Becoming **manic** about meditation is also common. You're so excited you can't contain yourself. It's great if you're excited, but don't get too carried away. Meditation is not a panacea, so don't burden it with unreasonable expectations. The middle-way approach is always best. Use your excitement to get the ball rolling, but temper it by being realistic.

Laziness is always an issue. After an initial flurry of interest, the fascination wears off. Laziness also comes in two forms. The first is the ordinary "I can't be bothered" variety. I'd rather go for a walk or take a nap. The second is sneakier. This is active laziness, which is about jamming our lives with so many activities that there's just no time to meditate.

Laziness is an expression of our resistance, which can also manifest in thinking and talking about meditation instead of doing it. This is when we need to reflect on why we were interested in meditation in the first place. Think about it, and think about it deeply. Is your distracted life bringing you the happiness you seek, or fulfilling the deeper aspirations you have for your life? Do you want the rest of your life to look like the first part? Are you willing to do a little work to acquire inner peace? Then remember that meditation is a practice. Nothing worthwhile is ever accomplished without effort.

Near enemies

While there are many noble qualities that develop in meditation, there could also be darker elements. Wherever there is light you will find shadows. Lurking in the shadows are a host of near enemies. These are sinister characteristics very near to the good qualities, but that often derail them. They are so close to the qualities that we don't see them. For example, the near enemy of compassion is pity, the near enemy of confidence is arrogance. Once you become sensitized to the idea of near enemies you will start to find them. They're just ego's way of twisting something good, which makes it go bad.

Touchiness and irritability are near enemies to the heightened sensitivity that develops in meditation. There's a beautiful teaching that says you can get so open that it hurts when a leaf hits the ground. Meditation wakes you up and makes you more open and aware. It breaks down crusty barriers, opens your heart, and allows you to feel more. You may find yourself more available, even vulnerable, to the feelings of others. Things start to get to you. This is a noble quality that gives birth to empathy and compassion.

I'm often moved to tears by watching a sentimental commercial or human-interest story. At first I was embarrassed to be so sensitive. Now I celebrate it.

But there are times when I get touchy. Sounds get to me. Traffic sometimes annoys me. I can get fussy. This is the shadow side of being so open. We all have these feelings, of course, but I notice they tend to increase with meditation before finally decreasing. They may increase as our sensitivity increases, but then decrease as our meditation matures. With continued practice we become more accommodating to these irritations.

If you relate to these touchy feelings properly they're never a big deal. Notice the irritability, and make friends with it. Realize that you're human and doing your best. I find that I get irritable when my mind gets small. The tiniest things get big if I put them in a small container. Put a teaspoon of salt in a shot glass and you've got some nasty water. Put that same spoon of salt in Lake Michigan and it has no effect.

These bothersome feelings are like annoying guests at a hotel you own. You don't have to indulge them, but you do need to host them. Give them space. They'll temporarily check into your mind but they always check out.

Meditative bypassing is a near enemy to the natural distancing that develops in meditation. This is a more sophisticated problem, one that has wider implications and more damaging consequences. As we've seen, meditation infuses a quality of space into your mind. It provides new perspectives on what happens in your mind, and by extension, your life. This perspective prevents you from getting sucked into, and then overly involved with, thoughts, emotions, and life situations.

But this spaciousness can slide into various forms of spaceyness. Healthy distance slips into pathological distancing. Instead of using your new perspective to help you see things more clearly, you may use it to avoid things. That's the bypassing. Instead of relating to thoughts and emotions properly, you slip into repressing or shunning them. Instead of becoming more responsible for what happens in your mind and life, you end up shirking your responsibilities.

Another aspect of meditative bypassing occurs if you put too much emphasis on your formal sessions. You could be using meditation as an escape. This usually doesn't happen with beginners, but with intermediate or advanced meditators. Escapism occurs when healthy renunciation, a key ingredient on many spiritual paths, slips into the near enemy of rejection. For example, it's good to renounce excessive involvement with materialism, but not so good to reject everything material.

One way to detect meditative bypassing is to see how you respond when your meditation is interrupted. If you get irritated when something or someone barges into your meditative space, something may be off. You might be getting territorial with your meditation, using it to avoid the everyday challenges of life. You do need to protect your meditation sessions, otherwise daily distractions will stampede over them, and you need discipline and the courage to set boundaries: "No, I can't do that right now. I have a meditation session. I can do that later." But be careful how defensive you get about practice. Meditation is about opening to your mind and world. If you find yourself shutting down, find out why.

Many people take up meditation because they're unhappy. They want to reduce the speed and stress, which they associate with daily life. For most of us this means taking a vacation. Vacations are great, but if that attitude is brought to your meditation, it can turn into an exit strategy, which is another form of meditative bypassing.

Meditation should only be an escape, or tool, to get us out of our inappropriate relationship to thoughts, things, and emotions. It provides an elevated perspective and allows us to perceive the world in a new light. But this perspective is not demeaning. Thoughts and emotions are not belittled in this regard. They may shrink in importance, but they're always held in proper perspective. Meditation allows you to transcend excessive involvement with thoughts and emotions, yet maintains their importance for functioning in the world. Respect the contents of your mind, just don't buy into them. Use them, don't let them use you.

So the near enemy of an elevated view of thoughts and emotions is one that puts them down, in a negative sense. Instead of just dropping them when we label them "thinking," it's like we then step on them. If we're not careful, this dismissive attitude to thought can turn into anti-intellectualism, or a condescending view about science and rationality. Thoughts are the natural play of your mind. There is no need to stomp on that play.

Remember that one of the switcheroos in meditation is that it doesn't lift you up and out. It drops you down and in. It's not an escape from reality, but a descent into it. This is important because many people think that meditators just sit around and "stare at their navels." Some people do use meditation like a drug or a sedative, to escape from their problems. But real meditation invites a return to reality, and all the worldly responsibilities associated with it.

Another indicator of meditative bypassing is a sense of judgment, even a belittling attitude, towards non-meditators. If you find yourself feeling superior, that you've got the goods and non-meditators do not, you're starting to use meditation as a credential and a shield. The point of meditation is to break down boundaries, not build them. So be wary of these subtle traps.

As with any problem, awareness of it is half the solution. Just being aware of meditative bypassing can help you prevent it. If you find yourself avoiding worldly responsibilities in favor of your transcendent meditation, come back to earth. This is another reason we spent so much time with the posture phase of meditation. Being with your body helps you stay grounded.

CHAPTER 12

Meditation and Children

I in twenty years as a meditation instructor, I have given talks to every age group, from toddlers in pre-school to the elderly in hospice. Introducing meditation to children is a delight—if not a challenge! It forces me out of my pre-conceived notions about meditation, and compels me to tune into the kids. That requires that I get out of myself and into them. If you don't listen and meet them where they are, meditation will fly right over their heads. Don't aim for their heads. Aim for their playful hearts and squirmy little bodies.

I don't have children, so my knowledge comes from teaching kids in settings other than my home, from meditating friends who have kids that I hang out with, and from books. Kerry MacLean, author of a number of delightful books on meditation for kids, says:

> As parents we teach our children to care for their physical well-being by brushing their teeth, eating right and getting enough sleep, but we aren't quite as clear when it comes to teaching them how to maintain their mental health. Children are so impressionable that even just two minutes of sitting meditation a day helps them learn

to self-settle and self-soothe. When kids have a peaceful place inside themselves, they naturally become happier and more positive, getting along better with one another and others in their world. Everyday obstacles become more workable and natural harmony is easily regained.[30]

Here are some guidelines for how to introduce meditation to children:

First of all, meditation is not for every child, just as it's not for every adult. Some kids take to it, others do not. Never push the issue. Just because you're passionate about meditation doesn't mean your child will be. I have friends who are lifelong meditators, and their children never developed an interest. Kids have to be willing to play with meditation. If they're not, wait. They may develop an interest later. If they don't, drop it. Love them just the way they are. Anything but the gentlest invitation can backfire.

It's difficult to teach your child any life skill *you* don't already have, so one of the most important things is for you to develop your own understanding and practice. In a beautiful way, you can "use" your child to help you further develop your own meditation. To share meditation with your kids, you need to know the essence of what you're sharing. You can't use standard adult terms like "label your thoughts," or "establish a relationship to your mind." You have to translate your understanding into their terms. So use the opportunity to teach them as a way for you to learn.

Children absorb the energy of their environment. If you create a peaceful and meditative space, either a physical space like a meditation room, or the spiritual space of your own heart-mind, it will naturally affect your child. This unspoken atmosphere infuses your home, and your kids will start to pick up the scent. Non-verbal approaches are among the best ways to introduce kids to the sweetness of meditation.

---

30 See www.familymeditation.com, accessed June 13th, 2013.

Kids often love to imitate their parents. Do it yourself and your kids may want to do it with you. I recommend parents do two types of sessions, one for themselves and one for their kids. If you want to go deep into your own meditation, you may need to practice before they wake up, or after they go to sleep. Otherwise they can interrupt your practice. If they do, never chide them. You don't want children to associate meditation with difficult emotions. Gently invite them into your space, just as you would any thought that may barge into your mind. The second type of session is for them. Now they can have your undivided attention as they explore cultivating their own.

Amy Hamilton, who wrote a book with forty-nine guided meditations for kids, *Indigo Dreaming; Meditations for Children*, offers these guidelines:

- Don't expect too much
- Be relaxed and calm yourself
- Keep your language and instructions simple
- Let them participate voluntarily
- Make it fun and enjoyable
- Explain to your children how good it is for them. That it improves memory, helps them to concentrate, etc.
- Tell them that it's like exercising their brain

Learning styles

Kids learn differently, so instruction isn't a "one-size-fits-all." Tune into your child and let their learning style guide you. Some kids are auditory learners, which means they work well with sounds and words. Guided meditations are great for them. I like Amy Hamilton's book because it's so imaginative and playful with guided meditation. Here are the names of some of her forty-nine meditations: Tree house; Super Hero; Secret Cave; Snow City;

Shining Star; Wizards Potion; Sleeping cloak; Circle of Light; Bubble Bath; Affirmation Box.

Others are visual learners. If you're doing a breath meditation you could say, "Take a slow deep breath, fill up like a balloon, now follow your breath out as it buzzes like a bee." The "muddy jar" analogy used earlier would work well with a visual learner, as do some of the picture books on meditation. (I ended up using a powdered metal, something that sinks and settles to the bottom quickly. Sand or dirt keeps the "mind jar" muddy for a long time). You could use other visual analogies, like the diving story in Chapter Three. If you live near a body of water, you could tell them that thoughts are like ripples and waves, and meditation is like the still water below.

Still others are kinesthetic learners, which means they connect best to bodily feelings. Invite them to feel the movement of their belly or breath as they breathe. For kinesthetic learners I like to do the "gathering the mind" movement discussed earlier. Demonstrate it first, and then invite them to join you. Sit down and close your eyes (this helps you feel into your body). Take three slow breaths to settle the mind, focusing on the expansion and contraction of the belly. Slowly stretch your hands out to your sides, and then bring your outstretched arms up over your head until the palms touch. With your palms joined, slowly bring your hands down till they rest in front of your heart, as if you were praying. Now guide them through it. Ask your child what this feels like. Using your own words, ask them if it makes them feel centered. Does it feel good as their hands rest in front of their heart? They may not feel anything, so don't expect too much. Invite them to explore what they feel, and then to share their feelings.

What works for one of your kids may not work for another. To be a good meditation instructor you have to be a good listener. Children develop personalities early. Some are introverts, and have a talent for introspective things like meditation. Others are extroverts, and may not have the capacity or interest for introspection.

Give them plenty of space to ask questions as they meditate with you. Allow them to modify the meditation, and to do what works for them. You might be surprised at what they teach you! Flexibility and humor are important. Don't take it too seriously, and don't impose anything. If it's more like a game they'll have fun with it and want to do more. If you impose your version of meditation you risk losing them.

Until they reach seven or so, guided meditations tend to work best. It's like telling them a story. Kids love stories, so create a good one that leads them into themselves. It's a great way to use their natural powers of imagination. By capturing their imagination you're capturing their attention. That's the trick. On one level, meditation is about capturing the wandering mind and returning it to the present moment. But capture doesn't mean arrest. So don't be too tight.

If a guided meditation, like a bedtime story, becomes their favorite, then use that. If they get bored with that story, find another one, or develop your own.

Short is sweet

If there was ever an application for short meditation sessions, this is it. Generally, the younger the child the shorter the session. How short? That depends on your child. Two to three minutes is a workable starting point, but it could be shorter or longer. Some teachers recommend one minute for every year, which means a five year old would meditate for five minutes, a six year old for six etc. You can stretch yourself into longer sessions, but don't stretch your kids, unless they ask for more. Err on being too loose.

Here's a short "gong" meditation you can do for young kids. If you have a meditation gong, singing bowl, wind chime, or bell, strike it and have your child focus on the sound. Ask them to raise their hand when they can no longer hear it. This invites them to pay attention in a playful way. Smaller gongs have shorter reverberations, bigger gongs hum longer. If you happen to have several sizes of gongs or bells, that's a fun way to play with this "gong show" meditation. Play with how hard you strike the gong, or hit it several times to generate a longer sound. Ask them how they feel after the sound fades into silence. Do they prefer the sound, or the silence?

I like "listening meditations" with kids. It forces them to quiet down in a gentle way, and to tune into their senses. Ask your child to sit and simply listen with you. Have them share what they hear. Do they hear that distant jet, or barking dog? You can have a fun contest where you both name all the things you can hear. Whoever hears the most wins. It goes without saying that you should almost always let them win.

Meditation texts use phrases like "look at your mind," and we have talked about "stop and see." Vipashyana, after all, is a term that means "clear seeing." I don't think enough emphasis is placed on "clear listening," or "stop and listen." I often listen to my mind more than I look at it. Deep listening forces me to quiet my mind. Listening to myself in this fundamental way helps me listen to others. Play with this idea with your child, and see if it speaks to them.

Be careful how you connect meditation to things like a "time out." "Time out" is a disciplinary measure, and even though there are obvious similarities between a time out and a meditation session, you don't want the child to associate meditation with that level of discipline. They won't meditate if it's not fun. If you can't find a way for them to enjoy it, then drop it. Try again when they're older.

Another tip is to invite them to meditate with you after they get up, or before sleep. Young minds tend to be more settled during those times, and easier to work with. Don't expect them to sit with you when they're bouncing off the walls. Respect their natural rhythms and tune into them. Kids also love ritual and repetition, so take advantage of that. They can look forward to meditating with you at the end of each day just as much as they look forward to reading bedtime stories.

Your child may respond best to meditating while lying down or walking. You don't have to sit to meditate, even though that seems to be the best general posture. Invite them to lie down with you, rest their hands on their belly, and count to twenty-one with you. Count out loud together, then experiment with dropping down to a whisper, and then see if they can count mentally. Experiment with a "mantra," which could be any special word you like. Try a single word like "peace," "quiet," "stillness," a religious world like "Jesus," "Buddha," "Krishna," or a short phrase like "love your mind," or "silent mind happy mind."

Empower their participation by inviting them to come up with their own special word. Try starting the recitation slightly faster and louder (to meet their speedy minds), then gradually slow down and quiet down. This decrescendo can drop them into stillness. After you've played with a number of techniques—guided meditations, mantras, or any other suggestion listed here—ask them what they want to do for "meditation time." You might be surprised what they like, or create.

Meditation for kids below seven

How early can a child be introduced to meditation? There's no standard rule. On one level, children can be "introduced" to meditation while they're still in the womb. There's anecdotal evidence, and some scientific studies, that suggest a meditating mother helps her developing child.[31] This makes sense, since meditation works to reduce harmful stress hormones. Once a child is born, further levels of "atmospheric" introduction can be made by having the infant sit in your lap while you meditate. This meditative holding environment will naturally extend towards your child. How much it may influence their interest or ability in meditation is impossible to say.

Generally, kids won't be able to understand the concept of meditation before age seven. For really young kids, a "show and tell" approach, or simple imitation, is enough. The guided meditations of Amy Hamilton work wonderfully for this age group.

You might try basic sensory awareness, or simple body scans, with really young kids. Invite them to explore their body by lying down. Then ask them to feel their feet, their calves, knees, thighs etc. This helps them ground their awareness into their bodies in a playful way. You can start the series, then ask them to take over and guide you as you both work your way up or down the body. Some kids are competitive, so I'll tap into that quality. For example, I might say: "Okay, let's have a contest. Who can sit still the longest!" I'll sit next to the child and off we go, or in this case off we don't go. If I feel the child is getting too competitive and tightening up, I always let them win by moving first. Be careful not to get too competitive yourself!

---

31 See *Attention Deficit Hyperactivity Disorder in Children and Adolescents,* edited by Somnath Banerjee, published online June 2013. Chapter Four: *Is ADHD a Stress-Related Disorder? Why Meditation Can Help,* by Sarina J. Grosswald.

You can do a "countdown" meditation every night as you snuggle in bed, counting ten breaths or so. Or try the "stoplight" "stop sign" mini-meditation, which is good for everybody in the car. Every time you pull up to a stoplight you can say "Stop light meditation!" and everybody has to be quiet until the light turns green. If it's a stop sign, everybody is quiet till the car starts to move again. This is a great way to extend meditation into daily activity. If things are getting speedy around the house, you can play a "freeze" meditation. Set up the rules of this meditation game in advance by saying that anytime anyone says "freeze!" the rule is to stop whatever you're doing and hold that posture for a few seconds.

I've even heard of parents "bribing" their kids, always in a playful mode. "If you sit with me for five minutes, I'll give you a treat." This may raise the eyebrows of some meditation instructors, but when it comes to kids I tend to loosen up and have fun with meditation. You may discover that your own practice will be enhanced with these mini-meditations and games. They're a terrific way to expand your practice into life.

Other instructors have their own styles of teaching kids, and I'm confident you can develop your own. Coming up with new ideas will challenge you to deepen your own understanding. You will discover, yet again, that simplicity rules the day when it comes to meditation. In my opinion, if it works, do it. Kindness, love, playfulness, patience, and delight are the most important guidelines. If you construct your own techniques with these building blocks you'll be okay.

I like teaching kids because it forces me to be creative, and to have fun with a practice I often take too seriously. I continue to be amazed, educated, and humbled by the wisdom of children.

CHAPTER 13

Frequently Asked Questions

Why is meditating so hard sometimes?

While there may be part of us that wants to be mindful and aware, there's a big part that prefers mindlessness and unawareness. It's the power of habit again. Part of us loves to feast on fantasies and reveries, to languish in wild discursive thought, and to soak in images of the past or future. There's comfort in our fantasies, born from familiarity to these mindless states, that just feels good. It's like the comfort of a worn out sweater we just can't throw away.

We may know about the power of being present, and that it's good for us, but we also enjoy being absent, even though we know it's not as good. It's fun to space out or drift into a daydream. Like smoking, drinking, or eating junk food, it's not so easy to stop. There's a lot of resistance to just being here now. This is because there is no guarantee of comfort in nowness, which can be unpredictable and unsettling. We enjoy predictability, certainty, and comfort, and we never know what we'll find when we touch into the fleeting present moment. Recognize the resistance, understand where it comes from, and make friends with it. This "friend" will be with you for a long time.

Remember that any discipline requires effort. Especially if it's new and unfamiliar. You're going against a tidal wave of distraction and speed, so be patient. It could also be hard because you feel you can't do it, or still think that you're a bad meditator. When I first started meditating I thought I was horrible at it. Looking back I now realize it was hard because I had a warped definition of meditation, one that I couldn't live up to. Anything is hard if you're hard on yourself. Review the sections in this book that deal with this obstacle, and be kind to yourself.[32]

Is meditation dangerous?

Some people are afraid of what they might find when they meditate. Uninformed critics say that demons lurk within, and that meditation can unleash the devil. That's just silly. While meditation isn't always easy, it is safe. You will not go mad or become psychologically disturbed. You may lose your selfishness, your arrogance, or your pettiness, but if meditation is performed properly and supervised with a competent instructor, you will not lose your mind, or yourself, or who you really are. If you're seeing a therapist or psychiatrist and concerned about the place of meditation in your life, consult with them before you begin meditating. It's possible that meditation could be contraindicated in some dissociative disorders or psychiatric conditions.

Instead of losing your mind, you may find your true self, and discover that it is fundamentally good. Look deep within and you will find beauty, love, and the noble qualities of the enlightened mind and heart. People may be nervous about meditation only because they're not familiar with it. We're always anxious about things we don't know. But once you become familiar with

---

32 In *The Power and the Pain: Transforming Spiritual Hardship into Joy,* I spend a lot of time on this obstacle. Fundamentally, meditation is only as hard as you are. See p. 37-49 of *Power and Pain.*

meditation, there's absolutely nothing to be afraid of. With a proper understanding, there's so much to look forward to.

Meditation is as natural as air or water. Remember that meditation doesn't introduce anything new, it simply nurtures qualities we already have. But anything can be abused if it's misunderstood, even if it's good for you. If you breathe too fast you can hyperventilate, if you drink too much water you could over hydrate.

Meditation is a prescription for kindness and sanity. If it's not "taken as directed," which usually means being too tight with the technique or trying too hard, it might cause unnecessary challenges. These are rare and easily remedied. It's hard to overdose on meditation. The problem is usually under-dosing. In all my years of meditating and instructing, I've never seen any danger with meditation if it's done correctly.

Meditation, however, should come with this warning label: it may be hazardous to your ego. But it's medicine for your spirit. Let's put it this way, it's a lot more harmful *not* to meditate.

Meditation calms things down, but it can also stir things up. If someone gets deeply into meditation it can cause good problems. Meditation can dislodge repressed issues and bring them up to the surface. Trungpa Rinpoche said that meditation isn't a sedative. It's a laxative. This may seem problematic at first because you may not want to face certain crappy things, but in the long run it's good for you. It's similar to having a symptom surface that helps you identify an underlying disease. If you don't recognize habits or subtle symptoms of an underlying illness, it can kill you. Ignorance is never bliss. Awareness is bliss.

Awareness is like a solvent. It can reach deep inside of you and dissolve almost anything. When it dissolves our overt problems, we celebrate its power. But it can also dissolve things we didn't realize needed to be dissolved, like our ego. Now matter how temporarily unsettling this dissolution may seem, it is healthy. If there's a fundamental cure for virtually anything, it's awareness, and the truth that it reveals. Even if it may not always be pleasant. Medicine doesn't always taste good, even though it's good for you.

Is meditation for everyone?

Yes and no. Yes, in the sense that anyone with a mind can meditate. No, in the sense that many people just aren't interested. As with exercise, people may know about the benefits of meditation but are too busy, lazy, or apathetic. If they happen to be your friends, be careful how you present meditation. Because of its connection to spirituality and religion, it's easy to come across as a proselytizer. Practice your own meditation, and people who know you may start to see the changes. If they do ask, speak from your heart. Let your mere presence teach them. Don't try to convert anybody to anything.

Will meditation solve my problems?

Because mindfulness can be applied to every moment of life, it's easy to think it can cure anything. Meditation is miraculous in its applicability and scope, but just being mindful will not solve everything. It may help you see your problems more clearly, and therefore identify issues that were previously invisible, but meditation will not necessarily cure them. Like a newly elected candidate for public office, it's easy to project all our hopes and dreams onto this unknown commodity. We want to be saved, and maybe meditation can save us.

A holistic or integral approach to human development is the best way to grow, and to deal with life. There is a vast spectrum of traditions—physical, psychological, and spiritual—that work with every aspect of human nature. Meditation can augment the power of these traditions, but it should not be used to supplant them.

For example, meditation is not a substitute for psychotherapy. It can support therapy, but don't drop your therapy for meditation. It's easy to get stuck anywhere in life, and lean too hard on meditation to solve your problems. Many people could benefit from psychotherapy. I work with therapists without hesitation and continue to find their counsel invaluable.

Is meditation a form of therapy?

While meditation is therapeutic, it is not a therapy. In other words, meditation may help to heal psychological wounds, and nurture healthy relationships, which are all therapeutic benefits, but it is not itself therapy. Many of the qualities that develop in meditation are similar to qualities that develop in psychotherapy. You become more aware, sensitive to yourself and others, and understanding. So while meditation easily blends into therapy, they are not the same.

Much of therapy is more process oriented. Thoughts and emotions aren't directly released in therapy, like they are in meditation. Your therapist might help you discover where certain thoughts and feelings come from (your past traumas, for example), and therefore help you develop a healthy relationship to them. In meditation, there is no such overt processing. When a thought or feeling arises, you don't engage it or work through it. You touch into it briefly then let it go. You keep it simple.

It's easy to slip into forms of psychological processing while you meditate, and there's nothing inherently wrong with that. You may find yourself trying to work through issues on the cushion. But if you engage your thoughts, try to track down their psychological origins, or work out their effects, you're not meditating. You may be ruminating or even contemplating, but you're not meditating. The point is to be aware of the similarities and differences, and not mix meditation with therapy. Pay homage to both disciplines by keeping them in their respective domains.

I'm on medications, and in therapy. Is there a problem with meditating?

If you're on medication for behavioral or psychological issues, don't alter the medication without consulting with your doctor or therapist. While meditation can help with many conditions like anxiety, depression, ADD, or ADHD, don't replace your medication with meditation without talking to a professional. You may find that meditation can reduce or even remove the need for some medications, but let that discovery arise naturally, and under the supervision of your therapist or physician.

If you're in therapy, talk to your therapist about meditation. If they don't meditate, and are unfamiliar with the effects of meditation, consider finding someone who is. Your meditation can support your therapy and your therapy can support your meditation.

As mentioned earlier, there are some psychological conditions that meditation could worsen, and times when meditation should be suspended. That's why it's good to have a meditation instructor, or knowledgeable professional to advise you.

It's just not working. I can't meditate. What can I do?

It's probably because you still have some distorted image or definition of what you think meditation should be. You're still trying to measure yourself against some ruler. Shift your view, drop the ruler, and be patient. As simple as meditation is, it takes time to get the hang of it. Once again, simple doesn't always mean easy.

As straightforward as the instruction is, it takes awhile to refine it, and to polish your practice. The legendary NFL coach Vince Lombardi once said, "Practice doesn't make perfect. Perfect practice makes perfect." If you're not doing it properly, you may be practicing your edited version of meditation, and spin into detours. Understanding what perfect practice *is* takes time—and practice.

"Perfect" is a tricky word in meditation, because it often denotes some ideal or goal. The last thing you want to do is put pressure on yourself to become a perfect meditator. Meditation is not about perfectionism in this sense. But at the same time, there is imperfect practice. You may think you're meditating, but maybe you're just hanging out, allowing yourself to get carried away by thoughts. Start your practice with a "perfect" definition of meditation, or at least a good working one. This means allowing yourself the space to be human, and therefore imperfect. The Zen master Suzuki Roshi famously said, "You are perfect the way you are ... and you could use a little improvement." It's the ideal comment about meditation and the human condition. Always remember that meditation is habituating to openness. On one level, the only thing that's perfect in meditation is space, and opening to it.

If you're struggling, take a break. Maybe you're too tight. If the saddle is too tight the horse will buck. Relax your approach and bring a sense of humor to your practice. Go for a walk. Let the natural world invite you into your natural mind. Look up at the sky, and mix outer space with the sky-like nature of your mind. Look at the ocean or a lake, and let that stillness or vastness invite you into your own stillness and vastness. Lie down on the earth, and use your connection to that stability to invite the stability of your mind.

For those who are serious about meditation, there's a deeper reason why it may not be working. Some traditions maintain that without a solid ethical foundation, meditation will be shaky. If you lie, cheat, or are otherwise untrue, it's hard to nurture true meditation. Meditation as proper relationship is another way of saying that meditation is about *honest* relationships. If you're not honest with others, how can you suddenly expect to be honest with yourself on the cushion?

This is another example of how meditation works with your life. It cleans things up. So if you're struggling on the cushion, take a closer look at your life. Align yourself to the truth and you may find your meditation comes into alignment.

Commitment and consistency are the keys to successful meditation. It's not how you might feel in any given session. There will be highs, but don't let them sweep you away, and there will be lows, but don't let them take you down. Relate to a "good" and "bad" session just like you relate to good and bad thoughts during a session. Let them come and then let them go. The best meditators are those who just do it. As the Dalai Lama says, "Never give up."

I do okay with thoughts in meditation, but charged emotions throw me. What can I do?

This is an important topic. Emotions seem to be in a league of their own, more powerful than mere thoughts. Trungpa Rinpoche talked about emotion as energized thought, or thought and energy mixed together. As with thoughts, emotions only have the power that we give them. Left alone, they always self-liberate, or dissolve on their own. So the irreducible instruction, which we'll explore below, is to put a "Do Not Disturb" sign on your emotions. Leave them alone and they'll evaporate quickly, like a snowball hitting a hot rock.

It's such an irony. We feel that powerful emotions disturb us, but the real problem is that we disturb them. We just can't leave them alone, and therefore allow them to self-liberate. We usually can't help but feed the emotion with our attention, which keeps it alive long after it should be dead. The following instruction is helpful for emotions that arise in meditation, and particularly for emotions in daily life. These tips are a way to bring meditative principles to everyday emotional upheaval.

Before we look at the mental side of this issue, here's a compelling physical fact. Physiologically, the biochemical component of an emotion is flushed out of your system within ninety seconds of the initial trigger.[33] This implies that if an outburst persists longer than ninety seconds, you're the one feeding it. You're fanning the flames of a match that would otherwise quickly go out. Instead of mindfully choosing to come back to the present moment, you're mindlessly breaking away from what's really happening, and choosing to sustain the upheaval. You've checked out of your body (which is in touch with what's happening, and whose natural wisdom has already released the emotion) and into your head (which is usually out of touch with what's happening, and whose confusion keeps the emotion alive).

This scientific fact is humbling. It provides a physical basis for a spiritual assertion: that left alone, emotions flame out rapidly. It has shown me that I always have a choice, and that I'm responsible for my own emotional suffering or happiness. When my boss does something that I fume about for hours, that simmering is not caused by him. I'm the one that keeps burning myself. That's my choice.

It's a rare being that can allow powerful emotions to self-liberate within ninety seconds, so don't beat yourself up if the upheaval persists. Ninety seconds should not be set as the new standard for emotional freedom. If the energy lasts longer, just do your best to relate to it properly. Responding (vs. reacting) properly to the emotion is what it means to be responsible (response-able) for your emotions.

---

33 See *My Stroke of Insight; A Brain Scientist's Personal Journey,* by Jill Bolte Taylor, Ph.D., Plume Books, New York, NY, 2006, p. 153.

Leaving a charged emotion alone to die a natural death is not easy. Because emotions are so energized we get swept away with that energy. We lose it. Self-liberation is therefore something we need to practice.

Outside of leaving it alone, what else can I do to relate properly to an emotion?

The basic principles of the meditation technique apply to any emotion, but here are some additional tips to help you manage the additional energy. First of all, the energy of any emotion is fundamentally pure. Emotion is just the electricity of life. We dirty the energy by polluting it with our secondary thoughts. For example, the energy behind anger is perfectly pure. If we could leave anger alone, we would find intense clarity as the essence of that energy. Things would appear sharp and clear, penetrating and precise. But we sully the energy by adding all our commentary, rationalizations, etc. This is also what keeps the emotion alive after its built-in expiration date.

Secondly, feel the emotion properly, which puts you in touch with its purity. Let the energy touch you. That's what makes you human. But don't let the energy burn you, or take control. That's what turns you into an animal. Proper relationship is a middle-way issue: don't repress the energy and don't indulge it. Ride the energy, don't let it ride you. Feel the energy, but don't let it *involuntarily* move you.

We get into trouble when we lose the ability to feel, but we also get into trouble when our feelings take control. You want to feel, but to then be *voluntarily* moved by those feelings. You want to be moved by your love for another, compassion for those suffering, injustice in the world, or whatever brings about movement for the benefit of yourself and others. That's what constitutes proper expression of the emotional energy.

When you relate to the energy, it's electrifying. When you relate from it, it can be electrocuting. In other words, there's a big difference between emotion and emotional upheaval. Emotions are pure, upheavals are not. Remember our discussion on "meditation is a downer," and all the problems associated with *up*heaval? Here's a gritty application of that principal. When you're in the midst of an upheaval, drop into your body, where emotions are felt, and emotion becomes the voltage of life. But allow that energy to *up*set you, by letting it blow you up into your head, and you transform a pure emotion into a dirty emotional upheaval. Stop the thinking and allow the feeling. Stay with the energy as it's felt in your body. That's how you purify an emotion.

I've spent a lot of time with meditation masters, and marvel at how they deal with emotional situations. The mastery comes from their ability to master their energy. These great beings are not emotionally dead. They live with emotional gusto, feeling everything. I have witnessed the most amazing emotional energy in these beings, but it always burns cleanly, leaving no trace.

Here's one technique that has helped me deal with emotional upheaval. When you're in the midst of an emotional upheaval, drop the object, person, or event that triggered the upset and stay with the raw energy of the emotion. Dropping the trigger, which is what keeps you up in your head, helps you drop into your body. Since emotion is thought mixed with energy, drop the thought—which keeps the energy from self-liberating—and you're left with *pure* energy.

I grew up on the shores of Lake Michigan and often swam in big surf. If a really big wave was coming, the best way to handle it was to face it directly and dive right in. If you didn't, the wave would smash you into the sand and throw you onto the beach all mauled up. Dropping into the emotional energy you feel in your body is like diving into the wave. Letting the energy carry you away into your head is like getting mauled on the beach.

Since anger is such a damaging emotion, let's use it as an example. Some jerk just about ran you off the road. Your heart is pounding and you're mad as hell. Instead of racing up to glare at the driver, flash your lights, or flip them off, allow yourself to feel that surge of energy. Feel your shakiness, your heart pounding, and the rush of raw energy. Don't send your mind out to the object, in this case the person who is suddenly a jerk. Stay at home with the feelings in your body. Feel into the seething energy we call anger, but without indulging it.

If you're in conversation with someone and feel your emotions taking control, slow down, or pause. Feel into the energy that is about to carry you away, but hold your seat. It's harder to drop the trigger point if it's in your face and you have to relate to it. But try to relate to it properly. Give the person space to express themselves, and give yourself the space you need to relate to your own energy properly.

If my girlfriend unloads on me about something and I don't react, or I *respond* spaciously with kindness and understanding, her energy goes into space and dissolves. I don't give it anything to hit. A fight is diverted. She may mumble to herself if she gets no reaction from me, and therefore keep *up* the fighting energy within her, but the energy liberates much more quickly if I don't help feed it. The trick is not to use this as a passive-aggressive strategy. It has to be done with kindness.

Anytime an emotion upsets you, during meditation or in life, it's helpful to stay with the anchor of your breath. Otherwise staying with the energy, without some lifeline, can consume you. Our habitual tendency to cave into the energy is overwhelming. Being mindful of your breath acts like a container that can hold the energy. It's as if you're holding the energy with space, which can contain anything. Bombs can go off in space and the space remains unaffected. You can't cut it, burn it, or hit it. If you can identify with the space, which your breathing invites you to do, while still feeling the energy, you will discover the immovable and even indestructible quality of your being. If you can do that, notice how quickly the energy will course through you and self-liberate. Because you felt it so purely, it burns itself out quickly.

It's hard to stay with emotional energy, and take responsibility for it, but it's more mature. Children, for example, rarely relate to their emotions. They almost always act out from them. Babies scream for attention, toddlers throw tantrums, behavior that would be unacceptable for adults. A definition of "childish" is someone who can't relate to their emotions.

It's helpful to practice working with emotions on your terms. What I do is sit in meditation, which acts as a crucible for emotional energy, and invite a powerful emotion. I'll think about someone who ignites a feeling, and then explore the energy as it bounces back and forth between the trigger point and me. I feel the energy in my body, and then the knee-jerk reaction to blow it up into my head. My mind is so quick to spin the energy into a cyclone of upheaval. It's not always a pleasant meditation, but it has helped me establish a relationship with basic life energy on my terms. Inviting difficult emotional energies into your meditation is a more advanced form of practice, but it can be a lifesaver—quite literally.

Meditation as Diet, Exercise, and Hygiene

In many ways our mind is like our body. For optimal health and happiness, they both need to be properly fed, regularly exercised, and frequently bathed. If we don't tend to our mind the way we tend to our body, it will get "fat, dirty, and sick." The result is unhappiness, or even mental illness. Good mental hygiene, mental nutrition, and mental exercise are one way to look at meditation.

The parallels between physical and mental health are striking. When I wrote this appendix I quickly realized the analogies were endless. Analogies are never the real thing, otherwise they wouldn't be analogies—they would be the real thing. But the degree to which hygiene, nutrition, and exercise apply to both body and mind is uncanny. Virtually any word that applies to physical diet, hygiene, and exercise can also apply to its mental counterpart. From a spiritual perspective this hints at their ultimate non-duality. On one level, they really aren't different. So to understand how meditation works with the mind, let's explore these similarities with the body. We learn new things by comparing them to things we already know. It's like this . . .

In terms of nutrition, the mind is always consuming things. We "eat" whatever we pay attention to. Experience is our plate, and attention is our fork and knife. In order to swallow something mentally or physically, the first thing to do is cut it into bite-sized chunks. That's what we've done with the chapters of this book. Each chapter takes another bite into meditation. Just like food, we smell it, taste it, chew on it, and eventually gulp it down. Then we see if it agrees with us.

Physically and mentally, we are what we consume. If we're exposed to love, kindness, and generosity, we will digest, metabolize, and eventually become that. We will embody those qualities. If we consume anger, hatred, and miserliness, we will become that. We only have to listen to the news to realize that something is off in our mental diets. We're being fed all kinds of junk food, and the result is an epidemic of psychic malnutrition, or rampant mental eating disorders. On my bookshelf I have a 700-page medical pathology textbook. Right next to it is an 886-page mental pathology textbook (DSM IV). A principal cause of so much mental and physical disease is what we put into our body and mind.

Information is the food of the mind. Not only are we consuming bad information, but because we live in the Information Age we're consuming too much of it too fast. Fast food comes in physical and mental forms, and both can lead to indigestion—physical or mental. We're just not digesting information properly.

Because most of what's out there is junk information, most of what we mentally consume is junk. We watch trashy TV, read junk mail, and digest literal or metaphorical spam. In my grocery store, the colorful candy section is right next to the colorful magazine rack. I see no difference in nutritional value. The result of a mental junk diet is mental obesity (a mind full of garbage) and dis-ease (an unhappy mind).

Meditation and contemplation are healthy diets for the mind. Instead of just gorging on whatever we want, contemplation restricts our mental diet. Instead of fast food, contemplation invites slow food. We cut out the sugars, fats, and artificial flavoring of experience and consume the fruits and vegetables. We elect to concentrate on the good things in the world. This doesn't mean we hide from reality, or deny the existence of bad food. It means we don't eat it. We choose to focus on what's good for us. We even say things like, "That experience really fed me. I feel nourished by this book."

Depending on how you look at it, and where you are on the meditative path, meditation is either a good diet or a fast. At first it feels like fasting. Anyone who has meditated for more than an hour will feel the thirst for distraction. You're sitting there following your breath, which may be entertaining at first only because it's different, but after awhile you lose your appetite for meditation and the hunger pangs arise for something different. In other words, you get bored. You're starving for stimulation. When the entertainment (nutritional) value of your thoughts disappears, you crave to fill your mind with something else. You can't wait to snack on a text message, nibble on an email, or devour an entire movie or book.

Boredom, as we've seen, is a good sign in meditation. It means you're starting to loose mental weight. You've seen through the false nutrition of distracting thoughts. If you can stick with this fast you'll become mentally lighter, more agile, and graceful. You become mentally quicker and more flexible because thoughts no longer weigh you down. A light mind is a free mind. This is part of what it means to become en-lightened.

Meditation only feels like a fast initially because most of the time we're on a binge. In other words, the contrast is more apparent at first. Because we're constantly gorging on daily distractions, feeding our mind whatever it wants, when we sit down and do nothing the mind feels famished. We're always chomping on fantasies about the past or future, or indulging our endless taste for entertainment, so when those are taken away in meditation, the mind starts to grumble. Like any dietary restriction, we feel the temptation to give in to bad eating habits. That "sweet indulgence" of a fantasy looks pretty good when you're starved for distraction. But sooner or later we realize the damaging effects of mental malnutrition (all those meaningless thoughts), and the nutritional value of the present moment.

From this point on meditation starts to feed us what we truly crave. We gradually lose interest in entertainment or distraction. We're no longer lured by the empty calories of the past or future because the present moment feeds us just fine. The fast has transformed into a feast.

The present moment then becomes the sustained diet of the meditative mind. Like any diet, it does require discipline and it can be challenging. But once you realize the benefits of proper mental nutrition, it's no longer a sacrifice. You realize it's good for you. Feeding on nowness becomes a natural and organic way of life.

This may seem like mere metaphor, or clever word play, but connecting mental and physical diets has practical implications. The mind is where the epidemic of physical eating disorders and obesity have their roots. Establishing an appropriate relationship to the contents of our mind, which again is one definition of meditation, can help us deal with the contents of our belly. Meditation is not a panacea, but it can help with any level of consumerism, physical or psychological.

Many people overeat because they feel some level of empti-ness, absence, or deficiency. They're hungry, but they're not sure for what. Since food is often the most available means to satisfy this ineffable emptiness, food is consumed. People eat to feel full, satisfied, and therefore content. But food is not the content that brings real contentment—in both senses of these words. After it fulfills its biological function, food becomes a substitute gratifica-tion. We abuse it to fulfill psychological, even spiritual, cravings.

Meditation is one way to satisfy authentic craving, what we're really hungry for, and to therefore help with one mental basis of obesity. The inexpressible emptiness that we feel, and that we fill with food or thought, is the emptiness of our experience. We of-ten feel that something is missing. As we saw in the introduction, something is missing. It's just not out there. Our attention is miss-ing. Our inability to be fully present is what generates the sense of absence—and our hunger. Instead of consuming experience fully with our total attention and participation, we barely sip on it, and then complain we didn't get enough. We didn't get enough because we weren't present enough.

Fill your mind and heart with your full presence and you may find every other aspect of your life getting full. Mental gratifica-tion can trickle down to physical gratification, and the lessening of any level of consumerism. This doesn't mean that every med-itator is thin and fit. It's just not that simple. But it does imply a deep connection between mental and physical nutrition. For a few other examples of this connection, which is beyond mere metaphor: therapy is often needed to help us metabolize or ex-crete undigested experience; in spirituality there is a three-fold process of embodying the teachings—hearing, contemplating, and meditating—or ingesting, digesting, and metabolizing teach-ings till they become us.

One final comment about fasting. Many meditation retreats are held in strict silence, which is irritating to participants who love to chatter. But silence is a form of fasting. Our desire to fill space with idle conversation is put on a strict diet. The stillness of our meditation posture is also a form of fasting, which curbs our insatiable desire to move at a physical level. This is why people struggle and squirm when they're silent and still. Silence and stillness reveal our near lust to fill space, which in this fundamental way, we do with our craving for movement. Look at the movements of your body, mouth, or mind and you will witness your constant need to feel full—mentally, verbally, or physically.

Exercise

Until we sit down in meditation, most of us don't realize how flabby our minds have become. The common indicators of an out of shape mind is that it's stressed, dissatisfied, or unhappy. The biggest indicator is that it's constantly distracted. The unfit mind can't sit still. It's always darting around, looking to be fed with one form of entertainment or another.

A fit mind isn't distracted. It usually stays on the track of the present moment. It's light and flexible, yet strong and stable. Because it's so light, it's quick when it needs to be. But this mind also has endurance. Like a marathon runner, it will stay with something until it's done.

Just like the body, it takes time to get the mind in shape. It took awhile to get fat, it will take awhile to get fit. The qualities that we need to get to the health club are also needed to get to the cushion. It takes commitment, perseverance, and effort. When we first start to work out, it's hard. We can't lift very much and get easily winded. We come back from the gym tired, and wake up sore. But with repetition and constancy we begin to notice the changes. We feel better, the pounds drop away, muscles we've never seen before begin to appear, and our strength and endurance increase. Because we're getting lighter there's new zip to life. Even though working out isn't always fun, the results are. It keeps us coming back.

While physical exercise is about working out, meditation is about "working in." Even though the direction is different, many characteristics are the same. The first one is the "working" part. Meditation requires it. You can't drop a fifty pounds in a week and you won't shed a distracted mind in a month.

Meditation can be challenging at first. We often can't sit regularly for very long and are easily distracted. We never knew we were so out of shape. It's easy to get discouraged. This is why it's helpful to meditate at a center, or with others. Just like working out with others at a gym can inspire you, working in with fellow meditators also helps.

Just like in exercise, with repetition and constancy we begin to notice the changes. We start to feel better. Distraction drops away, qualities of the mind we've never seen before start to appear, and mental strength and endurance increase. Because the mind is getting lighter, there's new zip to life. We take fresh delight in ordinary things. Even though "working in" isn't always fun, the results are. It keeps us coming back.

In physical exercise, you don't get fit by lifting 1,000 pounds one time, but by lifting a few pounds 1,000 times. Repetition and constancy are the keys to mental and physical health. If you're too ambitious in the gym, you can strain a muscle and give up. If you're too ambitious on the cushion and strain your mind, it's also easy to give up.

Once again, the theme of "not too tight, not too loose," helps. If you work out too much, you'll get hurt. If you don't work out enough, nothing happens. The middle way is best. Current research says that thirty minutes a day, four to five times a week, is a great way to get in physical shape. To get in mental shape, twenty minutes every day is ideal for many people. Physical or mental, it's interesting that it adds up to about the same amount per week. If you want to attain peak performance and reach an Olympic level of fitness, it obviously demands a great deal more time and effort. Similarly, if you want to take mental health to its peak it also takes a great deal of time and effort.

Analogies are only analogies. Even though there are many similarities between physical exercise and meditation, there are important differences. While mental strength and endurance are the fruits of meditation, as the mind gets stronger in meditation it also gets softer. So while the body gets hard and tough in exercise, the mind gets soft and kind in meditation. And while movement is good for the body, stillness is good for the mind.

Another difference lies in the role of effort. In meditation, we start with deliberate, or effortful mindfulness. It takes work to bring the mind back to the present moment over and over. This is the exercise part. But because mindfulness is a natural quality of the mind, at a certain point effortful mindfulness evolves into effortless mindfulness. It just happens on its own. So while effort is important at the beginning, the heart of meditation lies in re-laxation. It's the final irony of the meditative path: all this effort just to learn how to relax.

The other big difference is that as you get older, no matter how much you exercise, your body eventually breaks down. With meditation, unless biological factors interfere that predispose you to dementia or other mental illness, as you get older your mind continues to get stronger. The mind doesn't fade like the body. If you believe in reincarnation, traditions like Hinduism and Bud-dhism say that the qualities of a really healthy mind continues from life to life. A mind can get so fit and "light" that it transcends the material body. If that's true, then it brings an entirely new dimension and benefit to meditation. Complete mental health is one way to define enlightenment. This super fit, or enlightened, mind never dies.

Hygiene

According to many spiritual traditions, the world, just the way it is, is basically good and perfectly pure. Shambhala talks about "basic goodness," Buddhism describes "natural great perfection," Gnosticism speaks of "heaven on earth." With all the strife, pollution, economic hardship, and warfare, the world doesn't seem very pure. For most of us the view of basic goodness is naïve and simplistic. It's New Age mumbo-jumbo.

But strife, pollution, economic hardship and warfare only come about because we don't focus on basic goodness—on the way things really are. We don't accept the doctrine of innate purity, so we spend most of our lives trying to clean things up outside. This external impulse ironically stains reality and sends us in the wrong direction. In everyday life it gives rise to unhappiness. At its extreme, this impulse gives rise to things like ethnic cleansing and terrorism.

This external view sends us off course because the real issue is cleaning up inside. The dirt is in here. If we practice good mental hygiene, which is what meditation is about, we will discover that the world gets cleaner as we start to bathe. It's the great switcheroo, and a magical by-product of meditation. In a famous verse by the Indian sage Shantideva, "You can try to pave the world with leather, or you can wear shoes."

People tend to focus on filth, all the negative things in life. Getting the dirt on somebody feels good, and it sells. Gossip magazines sell. Gossip is mostly trying to get others to agree with our negativity. It's almost fashionable to complain, and to point out faults. The weather sucks, the economy is pathetic, and the world is going to hell. It might be raining, the stock market may have dropped, and there truly is suffering in the world, but if we only focus on the filth we're soiling ourselves. This is what it means to have a "dirty mind."

Mental hygiene refers to the fact that we always have a choice. We can elect to focus on the dirt in the world, or we can focus on its underlying purity. This simple choice has dramatic repercussions. It's the basis of misery or happiness, as in the story of that ninety-two year old woman in love with her nursing home (Chapter Two). Focus on the filth and you will drag yourself and others down. Perceive the purity and you will lift yourself and others up. The great psychologist William James said, "Reality is what you attend to." Attend to the dirt and you will always find it.

Because meditation works with attention, it can help us dis-cover a clean reality. Last week I took a flight to Los Angeles. The first part of the trip was bumpy, physically and psychologically. I had a hard time finding a place to park at the airport, the security lines were long, and the flight was packed. I ended up sitting in a middle seat in the very last row. I sat there, simmering in discontent, watching all these other people get on the plane— all of them with better seats. There was the overweight lady who needed to hit the gym, the scrubby guy who needed a shave, and the screaming baby who needed to settle down. And then there was me. The arrogant guy who was projecting all his garbage onto others.

When I finally caught myself, I was embarrassed at having soiled myself, and others, yet again. I closed my eyes, took a few deep breaths, and proceeded to clean myself up. I also caught the irony of having the seat right next to the bathroom.

When I opened my eyes I began to clean up the plane by re-membering the view of basic goodness. I made a conscious choice to attend to the goodness in others. I looked at the fat lady again and noticed the tenderness in her face. I glanced at the scrubby guy and saw kindness behind a weathered brow. I looked at the screaming baby and saw an innocent being hungry and afraid. And then I saw the arrogant guy who was doing his best to see the goodness in the world, but just forgot. I chuckled at the mess I had made, but took glee in how quickly I could clean it up.

As my attention shifted from perceiving the bad to seeing the good, my mood changed from misery to delight. I felt cleaner and lighter. My muddy mood was replaced with a fresh attitude. I showered off my sullied view of the world and uncovered a plane full of wonderful people. Reality is what you attend to.

Just like keeping your body clean takes repeated effort, sus-taining a pure view of your world also takes work. It's a practice. But the rewards are worth it. The practice of mental hygiene (what some spiritual traditions call "pure perception") shows us that we're not victims of this world. We're victims of our own dirty attitudes, and of what we attend to. The world cannot make us happy or sad. It doesn't have that power. Only we can do that. This is why some rich people are forever miserable, and some poor people are always happy. It's all a matter of focus.

And focus is virtually synonymous with mindfulness. This brings us to an important point. As critical as mindfulness is, mindfulness itself is fundamentally neutral. It's neither good nor bad. It's simply the quality of the mind to be fully present with what it's attending to. What the mind attends to is a different matter. That can be either good or bad.

Mindfulness is good in the sense that you're training your mind away from mindlessness, but one could argue that it's not inherently good. You can be mindful when you perform a life saving operation, or when you aim and pull a trigger. It's like tofu. Tofu by itself is tasteless. Soak it in a succulent French marinate and it becomes tasty. Soak it in kerosene and it becomes putrid. Meditation as marination has some validity.

This is why mindfulness alone doesn't quite do it. It's the root but not the fruit. Without mindfulness, nothing of virtue will grow. From this root we can grow the fruit of awareness, or the harvest of pure perception. In terms of mental hygiene, therefore, mindfulness is just the first step. First we cultivate the ability to focus. Then we can practice focusing on the goodness in ourselves, and others. In other words, basic goodness is a description of the purity of reality, but it's also a practice.

Mindfulness puts us in touch with the present moment, pure perception reminds us of its goodness. Pure perception is not blind and naïve. We still see the problems in the world. Indeed, we see them much more clearly. But we don't focus on them. We choose to focus on what's good.

Diet, exercise, and hygiene are three aspects of physical health that can help us, through the power of analogy, to understand the practice of mental health, the fruit of meditation.

Different Forms of Meditation

While our emphasis has been on mindfulness-awareness meditation, there are many other forms. Virtually every religion incorporates some version of meditation, and countless New Age and modern teachers have their own styles. The form of meditation presented in this book is a kind of ground meditation. It's common to many traditions. But as commonplace as it is, meditative practices are not "one size fits all."

Some people will connect to one practice and have no affinity with another. But mindfulness-awareness probably covers more bases than any other meditation. This does not lessen its profundity, but shows its vast applicability. It's one of the easiest meditations to learn. It's also one of the most time-tested and therefore proven methods. In teaching this form of meditation for over twenty years, I can safely say that it will work for you. When a meditation doesn't work, it's usually not due to the meditation. It's due to the lack of interest or discipline of the meditator.

But with that said, people are different, and therefore different meditations abound. Unless you have a strong aversion from the outset, I recommend that you stick with a meditation for at least six months to a year. Give it a reasonable chance. As with any other form of practice or training, if you don't stick with it, nothing will work. It's like the story of the man searching for water. He dug a six-foot hole in one location and found nothing. Feeling discouraged, he moved to a different location and dug another modest hole. No luck, so off to another location and another shallow dig. Instead of staying put and going deeper, his lack of perseverance guaranteed failure.

In this appendix I will discuss some of the most common meditations circulating in the West. Condensing entire traditions into a few paragraphs barely scratches the surface of what they can offer. Most of the meditations currently in the West are variations of the ones mentioned below. On one level, anything that slows you down and invites you to look within is a form of meditation. Some of the practices blur the line between contemplation, meditation, or even exercise. I will emphasize the meditative aspects.

Yoga

Yoga is perhaps the most widely used form of contemplative practice in the Western world. There are countless forms of yoga, ranging from the classical schools of Ashtanga, Iyengar, Kundalini, Kriya, and Hatha Yoga to the modern and sometimes controversial Bikram Yoga, Hardcore Yoga, Core Power Yoga, Pure Yoga, Hot Ki Power Vinyasa Yoga, Pure Prema Yoga, Restorative Yoga, Yin Yoga, Cardio Yoga, Music Yoga Flow, SLT (Strength, Lengthen, Tunes) Yoga, Mahayoga, YogaHop, and many others. At its best, yoga is a complete spiritual path. At its worst, it descends into competitive physical fitness or contortionism. For many meditation purists, it's debatable to even call yoga a form of meditation.

From a meditative point of view, yoga is a profound system for developing mindfulness of body. By engaging in the postures (asanas), the scattered mind is brought into the body and anchored there. I often come into a yoga session feeling disconnected and speedy. As I work into the poses, my mind settles into my body, and an hour or so later I leave feeling at peace. Yoga gently forces me into the natural wisdom of my body.

While genuine yoga, under the guidance of a qualified teacher, can be a complete path, from a meditative stance, it does have limitations. Even though yoga is a perfect practice for developing mindfulness of body, many would say that its ability to introduce mindfulness, let alone awareness, of the mind is limited. That's not what yoga is designed for. You just don't have the conditions conducive to fully settle the mind and then look at it.

While body and mind are not ultimately separate, for most people they remain so. Yoga works mostly with the body, meditation works mostly with the mind. The boundary is hazy, of course, which is why yoga is a fantastic preparation for meditation. By using the anchor of the body, yoga grounds the mind and prepares it for the practice of mindfulness-awareness.

Just to be fair, from a yoga point of view, meditation also has its limitations. If a meditator is sloppy in their practice they can spin off into an ethereal headspace, losing touch with their body and the world. They end up using meditation as an escape. Anything has its shadow side. The ideal practice is to blend body and mind, using yoga and meditation. In this way both disciplines strengthen each other.

There are also different forms of rhythmic breathing, or breath control practices, that are either directly associated with yoga, or closely allied with it. Working with breath is common in many forms of meditation. Even the generic instruction of counting ten breaths to control anger is an effective practice. There is an intimate connection between the movement of thoughts and the movement of breath, as we have seen.

Pranayama is an ancient form of yogic breathing, Sudarshan Kriya is a more recent technique introduced by Sri Sri Ravi Shankar. These methods show you how to use your breath to settle your mind, and to change the way you feel. The techniques release negative emotions, and purport to purify states like anger, stress, depression, fatigue, or anxiety. The breath is used to harmonize body, mind, and emotional energy, leaving the practitioner energized yet relaxed.

So is yoga a meditation? Yes and no. It could be viewed as a body meditation that can introduce you to more formal mind meditations. In my view, if something slows you down and turns you inward, it's worthwhile—no matter what you call it.

My own path of meditation began by watching the TV series "Kung Fu." As a teenager, I raced home to watch the actor David Carradine deal with the Wild West in a meditative way for fifty minutes, and then engage in some contemplative ass-kicking. I loved it. The idea of chopping my way to enlightenment worked for me. As silly as it now appears, at the time it was my way in. This Kung Fu master was centered, silent, and wise. I wanted to be like that. So if Hollywood can get someone onto the path, yoga or any another form of body-mind work surely can. My humble entry onto the meditative path has instilled tolerance towards the diverse paths that converge at the same introspective point.

T'ai Chi and Qigong

T'ai chi ch'uan, or T'ai Chi, literally means "fist (-fighting method) of the supreme ultimate." It is a Chinese form of meditation based on physical movements, and a method of self-defense. There are five principal styles, all of which involve the practice of slowly flowing movements that coordinate body and mind. It is said that these graceful yet powerful movements harmonize the energies of yin and yang, the feminine and masculine energies of the universe, that also reside within us, dissolve tensions in the body, enhance health, and remove blockages in our subtle energy channels (meridians).

T'ai Chi is similar to yoga in that it works with synchronizing body and mind. It's different in that the movements are more continuous, and it's considered a martial art. T'ai chi is performed slowly for health and meditation, or quickly for self-defense. It's another system to cultivate mindfulness of body. Because of the emphasis on the body, it's also similar to yoga in that it doesn't provide the conditions for working directly with the mind. Again, this is not a limitation per se. It's simply not designed to cultivate awareness of the mind, at least in the way we're defining it.

As with yoga, my practice of t'ai chi brings me into my body, and therefore settles my mind in a beautiful way. There's a sense of not only tuning into the wisdom and subtle energy of the body, but of harmonizing with the energies of the cosmos. In my travels to China, I'm always struck by the elegance and grace of hundreds of people practicing in the parks together. Just watching them settles my mind. While good for all ages, T'ai chi is especially easy for elders because many of the movements are gentle and rhythmic.

When I first tried t'ai chi, the instructor invited us to pair up for an exercise with someone near our own weight. We were told to stand behind our partner, wrap our arms around them, and lift them off the ground. Easy. Then the instructor told the person about to be lifted to direct their mind, and their chi (life force energy), into the earth. We were then told to try to lift them again. I'm pretty fit, and regularly lift weights. I was stunned when I couldn't lift my partner. By directing his chi into the ground, it was as if he bolted himself to the earth. When we switched places and I directed my chi into the earth, my partner could only get me off of my heels. It's this quality of grounding the mind, and developing a deep mindfulness of body, that makes t'ai chi a meditation.

Qigong, or chi kung, is another Chinese practice gaining popularity in the West. Many scholars consider t'ai chi to be a form of qigong. T'ai chi movements are performed as part of qigong practice, and qigong plays a role in training for t'ai chi. Qigong is a practice designed to balance qi (chi), the same subtle life energy involved in t'ai chi. Like t'ai chi, it can be viewed as an exercise, a meditation, and even an alternative form of healing.

Mindfulness Based Stress Reduction (MBSR)

MBSR is the blending of meditation, yoga, and medicine designed by Jon Kabat-Zinn at the University of Massachusetts Medical Center. It can be seen as *applied* meditation because it's designed to help people with chronic illness or stress. It's also a complementary form of medicine, one that is available in over 200 hospitals worldwide. More than 740 clinics, medical centers, hospitals and freestanding programs offer MBSR around the globe.

MBSR is an eight-week training program that cultivates awareness of the unity of body and mind. Countless studies have shown how stress contributes to disease. By learning how to manage stress through mindfulness, mental and physical disease can be managed, and even cured. MBSR teaches patients how to relate to their illness properly. Once again we have relationship as the core issue. Suffering is an inappropriate relationship to pain. In other words, while pain is unavoidable, suffering is optional. Relate to the pain properly and you can reduce or remove suffering.

MBSR points out how subconscious thoughts, feelings, and behavior can undermine physical and emotional health. While not a classic meditation per se, MBSR's great contribution is showing how meditation benefits body and mind. MBSR has spawned a number of offshoots, including Mindfulness-Based Cognitive Therapy, Mindfulness-Based Childbirth and Parenting, and Mindfulness-Based Relapse Prevention. With time, we will surely see "Mindfulness-Based" appended onto other human issues.

Vipassana

Vipassana is probably the most complex meditation to cover because it has so many different aspects. Even the word has different interpretations and applications. "Vipassana" is a Pali word that means "insight," and refers to insight into the nature of reality. So Vipassana meditation is most commonly known as "insight meditation." It's a principle Buddhist meditation with origins in India, Myanmar, Sri Lanka, Laos, and Thailand.

The Vipassana movement in America is pioneered by Jack Kornfield, Sharon Salzburg, Joseph Goldstein, Sylvia Boorstein, and Tara Brach. In Asia, some of the most famous teachers include S. N. Goenka, Mahasi Sayadaw, and Ajahn Chah. This form of Vipassana is part of the Theravada ("teaching of the elders") or Hinayana ("narrow vehicle") school of Buddhism.

Vipassana includes any meditation that cultivates insight, such as contemplation, analytical meditation, introspection, observation of bodily sensations, or even observations about life. Therefore the term covers a wide variety of techniques. It's fundamentally a practice of transformation through self-observation.

Vipassana is sometimes translated as "awareness," which means we have been talking about one form of it all along. In its broadest context, vipassana therefore refers to one of the two central pillars of all Buddhist meditation, the other being "samatha" or mindfulness ("shamatha and vipashyana" in Sanskrit). Even though there are similarities between our use of the term "awareness" and vipassana, there are differences in how this meditation is actually practiced.

Virtually every form of meditation can be categorized as *concentrative* (as in "to concentrate, or focus," as well as "to center") or *receptive* (as in "to be open, to receive"), or a combination of the two. "Concentrative" and "receptive" are modern ways of talking about samatha and vipassana, or one more way to discuss mindfulness and awareness. Concentrative meditations gather the mind. Receptive meditations then open it back up, and allow awareness to develop.

Because of its many forms, vipassana is difficult to summarize. Briefly: once the mind has settled via one of the four foundations of mindfulness—mindfulness of body, of feeling, of mind, and of mental objects (concepts)—you explore and gain *insight* into these aspects of yourself. This is why Goenka, for example, stresses the body aspect of vipassana, while others stress insight into the mind and its objects more directly. But either way, vipassana is an effective meditation that is gaining a strong foothold in the West.

Transcendental Meditation

I have a particular fondness for Transcendental Meditation (TM) because this was my first meditation technique, and one I still hold in high regard. TM changed my life. It showed me that I could experience a still mind—without falling asleep. TM was introduced in the 1950's by Maharishi Mahesh Yogi, the colorful and sometimes controversial Indian guru who became famous when the Beatles, and many other celebrities, began practicing TM. There are upwards of six million TM practitioners, making it one of the largest modern movements. TM, along with shamatha meditation, is probably the most widely researched form of meditation. Many publications proclaim its physical and psychological benefits.

TM is a form of mantra meditation, which means it uses sound as a way to gather the mind. It has its origins in Indian philosophy, in particular the teachings of Krishna, Shankara, and the yoga master Patanjali. A TM meditator practices twenty minutes in the morning and twenty minutes in the evening, and uses their mantra as a kind of funnel to gather the mind. The mantra is initially recited vocally, but eventually becomes a purely mental recitation.

Mantras usually don't have meanings, but derive their power from the sound itself. According to some sources, a TM instructor will give a student their mantra based on age and gender. However, the method for assigning a mantra is never discussed. Once the mantra is given, the student is told to never reveal it.

When I learned TM, I went to an introductory lecture and then met privately with my instructor. After making an offering to a shrine, I was introduced to my mantra, given instructions on how to practice it, and sent on my way. There were a few follow-up visits to refine my practice, but no ongoing training. These days TM is offered in a standard seven-step course, with much more follow-up.

Mantras are important in many meditations, and central to Tibetan Buddhism, which is sometimes called "mantra-yana," or "the vehicle (yana) of sacred sound." In the West, prayer beads, which are used to count mantras, are a popular fad. They are sometimes worn around the neck, or placed around the wrist. TM does not employ prayer beads, and students are not required to keep track of their recitations.

I still think TM is one of the most user-friendly introductions to meditation. While it has cultural trappings, it's mostly a secular form of mindfulness. At more developed stages, the mantra (the concentrative part) falls away and awareness (receptivity) can be cultivated. While I can't speak with authority on the advanced stages of TM, the fundamental principles are sound and the practice is simple.

One small issue I have with TM is its name. At its best, "transcendental" implies transcending our normal relationship to thoughts and emotions, thereby freeing us from them. But the term can also imply an escapist attitude, that meditation is about transcending reality. As we have seen, meditation is not about getting out of reality, but into it.

Tibetan Meditation

Because Buddhism is principally a meditative tradition, there are many forms represented in the West. We have already discussed vipassana. In this section we will look at Tibetan meditations, and in the following section we'll describe Zen.

Tibetan Buddhism is popular in the West. The Dalai Lama, Richard Gere, and Hollywood movies about Tibet have sparked an interest in this exotic tradition. There are hundreds of different forms of Tibetan meditation. In addition to shamatha and vipashyana, as well as mantra recitation, other Tibetan meditations emphasize the practices of loving-kindness, compassion, devotion, and visualization. Despite its esoteric aspects, Tibetan Buddhism is best summarized by the Dalai Lama: "My religion is kindness." Underneath all the cultural trappings is the basic message of waking up and helping others.

Loving-kindness meditation, or *metta* ("maitri" in Sanskrit) meditation, is found in many schools of Buddhism, not just Tibetan. The practice begins by cultivating loving-kindness towards yourself, and then extending that feeling to others. By reciting phrases like "may I be peaceful and happy," and "may all beings be safe and protected," one meditates on finding happiness in the happiness of others.

Tonglen, or the practice of "sending and taking," is similar. On the in-breath you visualize taking in the suffering of others, on the out-breath you visualize sending out love and light to others. It's a compassion practice, designed to open your heart and connect you to the world. Metta and tonglen blur the line between contemplation and meditation.

Visualization meditation, or deity yoga, is a more esoteric practice. It's connected to Vajrayana, or tantric, Buddhism. In this meditation you visualize yourself as an enlightened deity, and recite the mantra of that deity. In the Tibetan view, we're already enlightened. We just forgot. Our innermost being is already awake, which is what the word "Buddha" means—"the awakened one." Deity yoga helps us to remember. By visualizing ourselves in an enlightened form, we're waking up to who we really are.

Mahamudra and Dzogchen is getting a lot of press these days. These are among the most advanced meditations in Buddhism. They are formless meditations, which is what makes them so advanced. Instead of focusing on any object (form), the mind rests in formless awareness. They are the ultimate practices of relaxation, which is another reason they're so difficult. It's paradoxically hard for us to relax. While it's helpful to know about the philosophy behind these practices, don't rush to get to them. You can't get to graduate school without going through grade school.

Zen

Zen is one of the most popular forms of Buddhism in the West. "Zen" is the Japanese pronunciation of the Chinese word "ch'an," which means "meditation." There are two main schools, Soto and Rinzai. Soto Zen emphasizes basic sitting meditation, or zazen (za - sitting, zen - meditation). Zazen is a meditation that allows you to study yourself. It's largely a formless meditation, intended to free the mind from bondage to any thing, thought, or form. The point is to rest in a wakeful non-distracted state, where attention is not directed to any object, and therefore clings to nothing. In this state, your enlightened nature eventually reveals itself.

Rinzai Zen is famous for koan practice. Koans are the famous contemplative riddles, like "what is the sound of one hand clapping?" Paradox is central to koans because paradox is that which is "beyond" (para) "thinking" (dokein). Koans reveal the limitations of thought, and virtually force the student to take intuitive leaps into fresh insight. They can't be solved by reason, so in this regard they're not riddles. Solving a koan involves jumping to another level of comprehension. It's like intellectual jujitsu. The thinking mind is turned in on itself and short-circuits. The resulting gap in the mind allows a glimpse of one's Buddha, or awakened, nature to shine through.

Chanting

Chanting is a form of meditation that is common to countless traditions, from Gregorian Chants, to Tibetan mantras, Hindu liturgies, and Christian hymns or psalms. Drumming and gonging, which is also practiced by many traditions, falls into this general category of sound meditation. Sound is a commanding means for gathering the mind. It provides an audible reference point that invites and anchors the distracted mind. Chant "om" repeatedly and see what it does to your mind.

The outward effectiveness of chanting comes from its repetition, and the raw power of sound to instill resonance in the mind. The inner effectiveness comes from sound working on the subtle inner body, opening channels for the flow of life energy (chi, prana, lung). Hinduism and Buddhism both assert that the world is made of "sound," and therefore use sacred sounds to reveal that innermost world.

Chanting also includes the recitation of liturgy and prayer. Here it serves a dual function. In addition to the effects mentioned above, this form of chanting also delivers a condensed teaching. In many traditions, chants are recited every morning or evening as a ritual teaching. The message contained in these liturgical chants is so important that it warrants daily repetition.

Chanting centers and harmonizes the mind. Like other moving meditations, it is limited in its ability to cultivate awareness. When your mind is filled with sound, there's not much room for silent looking. Chanting does silence the noisy mind, but it's not so effective for discovering the deeper mind. In my experience, chanting is therefore a marvelous way to begin meditation.

Centering Prayer

Christian centering prayer has gained wide popularity in recent years, mostly due to the work of Father Thomas Keating. Centering prayer is about cultivating inner silence, through the medium of a "sacred word." Sacred words are like mantras in that they provide a center point for awareness. However, unlike mantra recitation, centering prayer is not an exercise in concentrating on sacred sound, but rather deals with intention. The idea is to maintain the intention, with the help of the sacred word, to open to God's presence.

Centering prayer is not a relaxation technique, or self-hypnosis. It's an exercise in faith, hope, and love. It's designed to cultivate a relationship with God, beyond mere conversation, and into full-blown communion.

Here is a summary of the practice:

- Sit with your eyes closed. Relax, and center yourself. Generate a sense of love and faith to God.

- Choose a sacred word that supports your intention to be in God's presence. Sacred words are words like Jesus, Lord, God, Savior, Mary, Father, Mother, Amen, Divine, Shalom, Spirit, Love, Peace, Mercy, Silence, Stillness, Calm. An inward gaze upon God may be more suitable for some people than using a sacred word. If so, the same guidelines remain for the sacred gaze as for the sacred word.
- Let that word be a symbol of your heartfelt intention to be in the Lord's presence, and open to His divine action within you.
- Whenever you become aware that you've been distracted, return to your sacred word (or sacred gaze).
- At the end of the prayer session, remain in silence with your eyes closed for a few minutes.

The minimum time for this practice is 20 minutes, ideally every morning and evening. You can ask the Holy Spirit to guide you in choosing a sacred word that's most suitable for you. Once a word is chosen, stick to it during the session. Don't switch to another word. During the course of the prayer, the sacred word may become vague, or even disappear. That's fine. On one level, the sacred word drops away as you become absorbed in God's presence. As you center yourself around the word, thoughts and emotions no longer have the power to distract. The sacred word, or gaze, then introduces you to the true language of God—which is silence.

Resources

www.meditationintheigeneration.com

This interactive website is designed to provide resources to build on what you learn in this book. It offers supplemental material not published in the book, along with suggestions on how to take your meditation to the next level. I'll share the latest research, articles on meditation, where to interact with other meditators, and help you find retreats to keep you engaged. As I prepare the forthcoming companion book on the benefits of meditation, you will be the first to receive excerpts from it, along with insights into how this journey will continue.

Guided Audio Instruction

Tara Brach, *Mindfulness Meditation* (Sounds True 2012)

Elisha Goldstein, *Mindfulness Solutions for Stress, Anxiety, and Depression* (Mindful Solutions, 2007)

Andrew Holecek, *Shamatha Meditation Instruction* (andrewholecek.com)

Jon Kabat-Zinn, *Guided Mindfulness Meditation* (Sounds True, 2005)

Jack Kornfield, *Meditation for Beginners* (Sounds True, 2004)

Thich Nhat Hanh, *Calm, Ease, Smile, Breathe* (Parallax, 2009)

Online Audio and Video Meditation Instruction

Talk and guided meditation by Jon Kabat-Zinn at Google's office: http://youtu.be/3nwwKbM_vJc

Mindful Awareness Research Center's Mindful Meditations: http://marc.ucla.edu/body.cfm?id=22

The Shambhala Sun Foundation's website for mindfulness: www.mindful.org

Sounds True's interactive guide to meditation: www.withinsight.com

UCSD's guided audio for MBSR practice: http://health.ucsd.edu/specialties/mindfulness/mbsr/Pages/audio.aspx

Online Courses

Duke Integrative Medicine: www.dukeintegrativemedicine.org

eMindful: www.emindful.com

Mindful Living Programs: www.mindfullivingprograms.com

Centers and Organizations

Shambhala International Meditation Centers (over 200 centers worldwide): www.shambhala.org/meditation/intro_programs.php

Center for Investigating Healthy Minds, Waisman Center: www.investigatinghealthyminds.org

The Center for Contemplative Mind in Society:
www.contemplativemind.org

Center for Mindfulness in Medicine, Healthcare, and Society:
www.umassmed.edu/cfm

The Mind and Life Institute: www.mindandlife.org

Duke Integrative Medicine: www.dukeintegrativemedicine.org

Garrison Institute: www.garrisoninstitute.org

Mindful Living Programs: www.mindfullivingprograms.com

Mindfulness Awareness Research Center: http://marc.ucla.edu/

The Penn Program for Mindfulness:
www.pennmedicine.org/stress

UCSD Center for Mindfulness: http://health.ucsd.edu/
specialties/mindfulness/Pages/default.aspx

Resources for Articles and Studies

Mindfulness Research Guide and Mindfulness Research
Monthly: www.mindfulexperience.org

The Center for Investigating Healthy Minds:
www.investigatinghealthyminds.org/cihmFindings.html

Greater Good: The Science of a Meaningful Life:
www.greatergood.berkeley.edu.

Mindful Magazine: www.mindful.org/mindful-magazine

Mindful: Living with Awareness and Compassion:
www.mindful.org

The Mindful Society: www.shambhalasun.com

Places to order meditation supplies

Samadhi Cushions: www.samadhicushions.com/ShambhalaSun

Dharma Crafts: www.dharmacrafts.com

Tibetan Spirit: www.tibetanspirit.com

The Monastery Store: www.dharma.net/monstore

Sharchen Imports: www.sharchen.com

Meditation apps

There are countless meditation apps popping up for iPhones and Androids that can help. When it comes to support for meditation: if it works, use it. Here are some links. I don't necessarily endorse all these products.

www.saturdayeveningpost.com/2013/08/14/health-and-family/tech/meditation-apps.html

www.fastcocreate.com/3024948/stop-think-breathe-tools-for-peace-creates-a-meditation-app-designed-to-promote-compassion

http://gadgets.ndtv.com/apps/news/new-meditation-apps-aim-to-lift-spirits-calm-the-stressed-out-474341

Bibliography

The Attention Revolution: Unlocking the Power of the Focused Mind, by B. Alan Wallace, Wisdom Publications, 2006.

Destructive Emotions: How Can We Overcome Them? A Scientific Dialogue with the Dalai Lama, narrated by Daniel Goleman, Bantam Books, 2003.

The Emotional Life of your Brain: How Its Unique Patterns Affect the Way You Think, Feel, and Life—and How You Can Change Them, by Richard J. Davidson and Sharon Begley, Hudson Street Press, 2012.

Everyday Zen, by Charlotte Joko Beck, HarperCollins, 2009.

Full Catastrophe Living: Using the Wisdom of Your Body and Mind to Face Stress, Pain, and Illness, by Jon Kabat-Zinn, 1990.

Fully Present: The Science, Art, and Practice of Mindfulness, by Susan Smalley and Diana Winston, Da Capo, 2010.

A Mindful Nation: How a Simple Practice Can Help Us Reduce Stress, Improve Performance and Recapture the American Spirit, by Congressman Tim Ryan, Hay House, 2012.

The Mindfulness Revolution: Leading Psychologists, Scientists, Artists, and Meditation Teachers on the Power of Mindfulness in Daily Life, edited by Barry Boyce, Shambhala Publications, 2011.

The Mind's Own Physician: A Scientific Dialogue with the Dalai Lama on the Healing Power of Meditation, edited by Jon Kabat-Zinn and Richard J. Davidson, Mind and Life Institute, 2011.

Peaceful Piggy Meditation, by Kerry Lee Maclean, Albert Whitman and Company, 2004.

The Shallows: What the Internet is Doing to Our Brains, by Nicholas G. Carr, W.W. Norton and Company, Inc., 2010.

Train Your Mind, Change Your Brain: How a New Science Reveals Our Extraordinary Potential to Transform Ourselves, by Sharon Begley, Ballantine, 2007.

Turning the Mind into an Ally, by Sakyong Mipham, Shambhala Publications, 2003.

Wherever You Go There You Are: Mindfulness Meditation in Everyday Life, by Jon Kabat-Zinn, Hyperion, 1994.

Acknowledgments

A deep thank you to David Berman, Dominie Cappadonna, Jeremiah Clark, Chris Thatcher, Paul Richards, Tom Roberts, and Laura Warner for insightful comments that helped shape this book into its final form. An ineffable thank you to Cindy Wilson, who was the nucleus of this book and the inspiration that brought it to life, and to Bob Wilson for his meticulous attention to detail. A universal thank you to the meditation masters who have touched my life, and inform every page of this book.

Made in the USA
San Bernardino, CA
23 April 2015